DATE DUE

Opinions on Church Music

COMMENTS AND REPORTS FROM
FOUR-AND-A-HALF CENTURIES

selected and edited by
ELWYN A. WIENANDT

The Markham Press Fund of Baylor University Press

Waco, Texas 1974

Library of Congress Catalog Number: 74-75229

Printed in the United States of America

A.M.D.G.

To Patricia, in appreciation
for her continued patience and understanding.

I challenge any one to say that he enters into a stately cathedrall and a barn, be it never so bigg, with the same temper of mind; for the former will strike a reverence, and raise the mind with a pleasure unknowne elsewhere.

Roger North, *The Musicall Grammarian* (1728)

Many people seem either to hold Church music to be an important branch of the musical art, and nothing more; or to regard it as only a kind of devotional exercise. The existence of two separate theories of Church music (the one purely musical, the other purely devotional) would be sufficient to account for the want of uniformity in the quantity, the quality, and the kind of music used in our churches — even if there were no other causes working to divide men on the subject.

R. B. Daniel, *Chapters on Church Music* (1894).

Preface

The place, importance, and purpose of Christian church music has been discussed since it was first introduced. It is not surprising that there has rarely been a common answer to its problems, either among denominations, communities, or even single congregations. The point in history when such discussion becomes a matter of general interest coincides with the emergence of the Protestant idea, for it is the decisions of the new thinkers that first show a divergence from the generally practiced rules that prevailed under an apparently universal catholicism.

As various Protestant attitudes were formed, the divergences of practice became more apparent. It is with the written evidence of such differences that this anthology is concerned. It is made up of a selection of letters, essays, sermons, memoirs, dedications, prefaces, and other documents, in complete or excerpted form, that shows some of the prevailing attitudes toward church music in each of the four past centuries, and in our own as well. The material is taken from the writings of musicians, critics, historians, clergymen, and the lay public, thus reflecting a wide range of reactions to the musical scene as it touches upon the church. The reactions of these writers will be seen to vary in many ways, depending on their religious bias, their musical knowledge, and the social conditions at the time in which their material was written.

The comments of Protestant writers form the greatest amount of the material, and this is inevitable for two reasons: 1) Protestants, being relatively untouched by long-standing traditions, have often felt impelled to justify or improve their religious practices and, fortunately, they have given rather detailed descriptions of their efforts, and of Catholic practices as well; 2) Catholics have rarely felt it necessary to give elaborate descriptions of what they felt was right and normal, and, likewise, they rarely displayed any interest in the alien activities of Protestants, although papal pronouncements shed an interesting light on the problems that Church had to face in adjusting to musical changes.

The compilation of these materials would not have been possible without the kind cooperation of the owners of copyrighted material. Acknowledgement is made at each point where their property is quoted. I want to express my appreciation for the efforts of the several librarians of the Crouch Music Library and Moody Memorial Library at Baylor University whose assistance and cooperation made my work much lighter. Publication of this volume is supported by the Markham Press Fund of Baylor University Press. My special thanks go to the administrators and editor, and to Lowell Browne for his advice and assistance.

Baylor University   Elwyn A. Wienandt
December, 1973

This volume is the second volume published by the Markham Press Fund of Baylor University Press, established in memory of Dr. L. N. and Princess Finch Markham of Longview, Texas, by their daughters Mrs. R. Matt Dawson of Corsicana, Texas, and Mrs. B. Reid Clanton of Longview, Texas.

Robert T. Miller
Chairman, Markham Press Fund
of Baylor University Press

Footnotes preceded by lower-case letters are from the original authors; those preceded by Arabic numerals have been added by the editor. Since there are no chapters in the usual sense, the numbering of footnotes begins anew with each selection.

The original spellings and punctuation have been retained in older materials, except when they cause an obvious distortion of meaning. Those few instances are marked, either by the use of brackets or a brief footnote.

Table of Contents

I
THE SIXTEENTH CENTURY

II
THE SEVENTEENTH CENTURY

III
THE EIGHTEENTH CENTURY

IV
THE NINETEENTH CENTURY

V
THE TWENTIETH CENTURY

THE SIXTEENTH CENTURY

Desiderius Erasmus

(1466?-1536)

A contemporary of Johannes Ockeghem, a choirboy under Jacob Obrecht, and a lifelong observer of the musical scene, Desiderius Erasmus (born Gerhard Gerhards), spoke out about musical practice a number of times. While he did not hesitate to praise music, his interest in the function of church music caused him to denounce branches and types of the art that seemed unsuitable. He criticized not only the loss of textual clarity, as in the passage quoted below, but also the intrusion of secular influences, as when he said, "the singing of hymns was an ancient and pious custom, but when music was introduced fitter for weddings and banquets than for God's service, and the sacred words were lost in affected intonations, so that no word in the Liturgy was spoken plainly, away went another [strand in the rope of tradition]."[1]

A Brief Comment about Church Music[2]

St. Paul says that he would rather speak five words with a reasonable meaning in them than ten thousand in an unknown tongue. They chant nowadays in our churches in what is an unknown tongue and nothing else, while you will not hear a sermon once in six months telling people to amend their lives. Modern church music is so constructed that the congregation cannot hear one distinct word. The choristers themselves do not understand what they are singing, yet according to priests and monks it constitutes the whole of religion. Why will they not listen to St. Paul? In college or monastery it is still the same: music, nothing but music. There was no music in St. Paul's time. Words were then pronounced plainly. Words nowadays mean nothing. They are mere sounds striking upon the ear, and men are to leave their work and go to church to listen to worse noises than

[1] J. A. Froude, *Life and Letters of Erasmus* (New York: Charles Scribner's Sons, 1895), p. 364. See also a passage quoted in Gustave Reese, *Music in the Renaissance* (New York: W. W. Norton and Co., 1954; rev. ed., 1959), p. 448.
[2] Source: Froude, *Life and Letters of Erasmus*, pp. 122-23.

were ever heard in Greek or Roman theatre. Money must be raised to buy organs and train boys to squeal, and to learn no other thing that is good for them. The laity are burdened to support miserable, poisonous corybantes, when poor, starving creatures might be fed at the cost of them.

They have so much of it in England that the monks attend to nothing else. A set of creatures who ought to be lamenting their sins fancy they can please God by gurgling in their throats. Boys are kept in the English Benedictine colleges solely and simply to sing morning hymns to the Virgin. If they want music let them sing Psalms like rational beings, and not too many of those.

Martin Luther

(1483-1546)

With the establishment of Lutheran practices in worship, there came the necessity to evaluate the function of music and to justify its place in the church service. Luther recognized a fact that has been apparent to men of every generation: that singing would not fill churches. One of his proposals was to plan everything to interest the young and the unchurched, for "with the others neither law nor order, neither scolding nor coaxing, will help."[1] One of the ways he hoped to interest his people was through the singing of hymns, and Luther's hopes were realized in later years as the chorale became an increasingly important feature in the elaborate musical settings that were performed by the choirs. Without familiarity to the congregation, the chorale verses would have carried little meaning; as it was, they served to synthesize and summarize the substance of the cantatas, Passions, and other works that accompanied or supplemented the services.

Luther's introduction to Rhau's volume[2] shows without any doubt that he was convinced of the efficacy of music in the church service. His comments here are largely confined to the validity of musical expression; in other places he devoted his attention to the desirability of retaining tunes from the Catholic tradition, modifying texts to the Lutheran ideal and, often, to the German tongue itself.

Preface to Georg Rhau's Symphoniae iucundae[3]

MARTIN LUTHER TO THE DEVOTEES OF MUSIC

Greetings in Christ! I would certainly like to praise music with all my heart as the excellent gift of God which it is and to commend it to everyone. But I am so overwhelmed by the diversity and magnitude of its virtue and benefits that I can find

[1]Ulrich S. Leupold, ed., *Liturgy and Hymns (Luther's Works*, LIII) Philadelphia: Fortress Press, 1965), p. 89.
[2]Walter Buszin, "Luther on Music," *The Musical Quarterly*, XXXII/1 (January, 1946), 81-82, describes this introduction as belonging to Rhau's *Selectae Harmoniae quatuor vocum de passione Domini*. However, Leupold credits the preface of that volume to Philipp Melanchthon. Buszin contends that Luther wrote both prefaces, and prints his translations of them with his article.
[3]Source: Leupold, *Liturgy and Hymns*, pp. 321-24. The translation is by Dr. Leupold.

neither beginning nor end or method for my discourse. As much
as I want to commend it, my praise is bound to be wanting and
inadequate. For who can comprehend it all? And even if you
wanted to encompass all of it, you would appear to have grasped
nothing at all. First then, looking at music itself, you will find
that from the beginning of the world it has been instilled and
implanted in all creatures, individually and collectively. For
nothing is without sound or harmony. Even the air, which of itself
is invisible and imperceptible to all our senses, and which, since it
lacks both voice and speech, is the least musical of all things,
becomes sonorous, audible, and comprehensible when it is set in
motion. Wondrous mysteries are here suggested by the Spirit, but
this is not the place to dwell on them. Music is still more
wonderful in living things, especially birds, so that David, the
most musical of all the kings and minstrel of God, in deepest
wonder and spiritual exultation praised the astounding art and ease
of the song of birds when he said in Psalm 104 [:12], "By them
the birds of the heaven have their habitation; they sing among the
branches."

And yet, compared to the human voice, all this hardly deserves
the name of music, so abundant and incomprehensible is here the
munificence and wisdom of our most gracious Creator.
Philosophers have labored to explain the marvelous instrument of
the human voice: how can the air projected by a light movement
of the tongue and an even lighter movement of the throat produce
such an infinite variety and articulation of the voice and of words?
And how can the voice, at the direction of the will, sound forth so
powerfully and vehemently that it cannot only be heard by
everyone over a wide area, but also be understood? Philosophers
for all their labor cannot find the explanation; and baffled they
end in perplexity; for none of them has yet been able to define or
demonstrate the original components of the human voice, its
sibilation and (as it were) its alphabet, e.g., in the case of
laughter—to say nothing of weeping. They marvel, but they do
not understand. But such speculations on the infinite wisdom of
God, shown in this single part of his creation, we shall leave to
better men with more time on their hands. We have hardly
touched on them.

Here it must suffice to discuss the benefit of this great art.[a]
But even that transcends the greatest eloquence of the most
eloquent, because of the infinite variety of its forms and benefits.

---

[a] Literally, "thing."

We can mention only one point (which experience confirms),
namely, that next to the Word of God, music deserves the highest
praise. She is a mistress and governess of those human
emotions — to pass over the animals — which as masters govern men
or more often overwhelm them. No greater commendation than
this can be found — at least not by us. For whether you wish to
comfort the sad, to terrify the happy, to encourage the despairing,
to humble the proud, to calm the passionate, or to appease those
full of hate — and who could number all these masters of the
human heart, namely, the emotions, inclinations, and affections
that impel men to evil or good? — what more effective means than
music could you find? The Holy Ghost himself honors her as an
instrument for his proper work when in his Holy Scriptures he
asserts that through her his gifts were instilled in the prophets,
namely, the inclination to all virtues, as can be seen in Elisha [II
Kings 3:15]. On the other hand, she serves to cast out Satan, the
instigator of all sins, as is shown in Saul, the king of Israel [I
Sam. 16:23].

Thus it was not without reason that the fathers and prophets
wanted nothing else to be associated as closely with the Word of
God as music. Therefore, we have so many hymns and Psalms
where message and music join to move the listener's soul, while in
other living beings and [sounding] bodies [b] music remains a
language without words. After all, the gift of language combined
with the gift of song was only given to man to let him know that
he should praise God with both word and music, namely, by
proclaiming [the Word of God] through music and by providing
sweet melodies with words. For even a comparison between
different men will show how rich and manifold our glorious
Creator proves himself in distributing the gifts of music; how
much men differ from each other in voice and manner of speaking
so that one amazingly excels the other. No two men can be found
with exactly the same voice and manner of speaking, although
they often seem to imitate each other, the one as it were being the
ape of the other.

But when [musical] learning is added to all this and artistic
music which corrects, develops, and refines the natural music, then
at last it is possible to taste with wonder (yet not to comprehend)
God's absolute and perfect wisdom in his wondrous work of
music. Here it is most remarkable that one single voice continues
to sing the tenor, while at the same time many other voices play

---

[b] I.e., for example, instrumental music.

around it, exulting and adorning it in exuberant strains and, as it
were, leading it forth in a divine roundelay, so that those who are
the least bit moved know nothing more amazing in this world.
But any who remain unaffected are unmusical indeed and deserve
to hear a certain filth poet[c] or the music of the pigs.

But the subject is much too great for me briefly to describe all
its benefits. And you, my young friend, let this noble, wholesome,
and cheerful creation of God be commended to you. By it you
may escape shameful desires and bad company. At the same time
you may by this creation accustom yourself to recognize and praise
the Creator. Take special care to shun perverted minds who
prostitute this lovely gift of nature and of art with their erotic
rantings; and be quite assured that none but the devil goads them
on to defy their very nature which would and should praise God
its Maker with this gift, so that these bastards purloin the gift of
God and use it to worship the foe of God, the enemy of nature
and of this lovely art. Farewell in the Lord.

---

[c] Luther uses the strong term *merdipoeta* to refer to Simon Lemnius, a humanist and poet who in the
same year had drawn the ire of Luther with a collection of poems slandering prominent persons in
Wittenberg and eulogizing the cultured, but profligate Archbishop Albrecht of Mainz; cf. *D. Martin
Luthers Werke: Kritische Gesamtausgabe* (Weimar, 1883-), L, 350-51.

Thomas Cranmer

1489-1556

Cranmer was Archbishop of Canterbury from 1533 to 1555, some of the most critical years of England's religious development. As advisor and sometimes toady to Henry VIII, manipulator of Edward VI, and victim of Mary I, he was in the forefront of Anglican development. His famous letter to Henry VIII was written three-and-one-half years before the Royal Injunction addressed to the Dean and Chapter of Lincoln Minster displayed the same concern over syllabic, clear setting of texts in English.

Letter of Archbishop Cranmer to King Henry VIII[1]

It may please your majesty to be advertised, that according to your highness' commandment, sent unto me by your grace's secretary, Mr Pagett, I have translated into the English tongue, so well as I could in so short time, certain processions, to be used upon festival days, if after due correction and amendment of the same your highness shall think it so convenient. In which translation, forasmuch as many of the processions, in the Latin, were but barren, as meseemed, and little fruitful, I was constrained to use more than the liberty of a translator: for in some processions I have altered divers words; in some I have added part; in some taken part away; some I have left out whole, either for by cause the matter appeared to me to be little to purpose, or by cause the days be not with us festival-days; and some processions I have added whole, because I thought I had better matter for the purpose, than was the procession in Latin: the judgment whereof I refer wholly unto your majesty; and after your highness hath corrected it, if your grace command some devout and solemn note to be made thereunto, (as is to the procession which your majesty hath already set forth in English,) I trust it will much excite and

[1]Source: John Edmund Cox, ed., *Miscellaneous Writings and Letters of Thomas Cranmer* (2 vols.; Cambridge: The University Press, 1846), II, 412.

9

stir the hearts of all men unto devotion and godliness: but in mine opinion, the song that shall be made thereunto would not be full of notes, but, as near as may be, for every syllable a note; so that it may be sung distinctly and devoutly, as be in the Matins and Evensong, *Venite*, the Hymns, *Te Deum*, *Benedictus*. *Magnificat*. *Nunc dimittis*, and all the Psalms and Versicles; and in the mass *Gloria in Excelsis*. *Gloria Patri*. the Creed, the Preface, the *Pater noster*, and some of the *Sanctus* and *Agnus*. As concerning the *Salve festa dies*, the Latin note, as I think, is sober and distinct enough; wherefore I have travailed to make the verses in English, and have put the Latin note unto the same. Nevertheless they that be cunning in singing can make a much more solemn note thereto. I made them only for a proof, to see how English would do in song. But by cause mine English verses lack the grace and facility that I would wish they had, your majesty may cause some other to make them again, that can do the same in more pleasant English and phrase. As for the sentence, I suppose will serve well enough. Thus Almighty God preserve your majesty in long and prosperous health and felicity! From Bekisbourne, the 7th of October [1544].

Your grace's most bounden
chaplain
and beadsman,
T. CANTUARIEN.

To the king's most excellent majesty.

Edward VI

(1537-1553)

In the second year of the reign of Edward VI, an injunction was issued, directing the officials of Lincoln Minster on the method of observing portions of the Service, especially with regard to the use of the vernacular and the cessation of antiphons to the saints and to the Virgin. The sense of the document reflects to some extent the letter of Thomas Cranmer. It is certain that the young king would not have issued any such order without the counsel of his religious advisors, among whom Cranmer may be counted.

The Royal Injunction of 1548[1]

. . . They shall from hensforthe synge or say no Anthemes off our lady or other saynts but onely of our lorde And them not in laten but choseyng owte the best and moste soundyng to cristen religion they shall turne the same into Englishe settynge therunto a playn and distincte note, for euery sillable one, they shall singe them and none other, . . . they shall euery Sonday Wensday and Fryday and fesiuall day in this Cathedrall churche afore the high masse in the myddyll of the chore singe thenglishe Letanye and Suffrages the same beying begunne of hym that executeth the high masse or by too of the olde vicars, and so done in order as yt is appoynted in the preface before the sayd Englishe letanye.

And also they shall haue the Epistle and gospell of the high masse redde every day in Englishe and not in laten. And the same to be redde euery day in the same place where they were accustomed to be redde on Sonedayes with such distincte audible playn voice as the chore and the standers by shall well vnderstande the reader.

---

[1]*Statutes of Lincoln Cathedral*, Henry Bradshaw and Chr. Wordsworth, eds. (Cambridge: University Press, 1897), II, 592-93.

11

Council of Trent

(Documents of 1562-1563)

The Council of Trent was convened on December 13, 1545, and finally dissolved on December 4, 1563. Its importance to music is often misunderstood and equally often exaggerated. But this is not to say that the Council failed to influence the course of further composition for the Church, or to change the method of performing works already in existence. Several sessions of the Council were concerned with music as part of the general problem of liturgical abuses. The Council made general recommendations about music without providing specific rules or restrictions. The way these recommendations were to be carried out was left to later interpretation and settlement by local authorities.

The Council did emphasize the importance of plainsong as a basis for proper music. Its simplicity, regularity, and abstract qualities were accepted as an ideal. Adaptation of widely differentiated local practices to the ideal were, however, too much to expect.

Rules for Sacred Music by the Council of Trent[1]

1. The Bishops and Ordinaries must prevent the use in Church of any music which has a sensuous or impure character, and this, whether such music be for the organ or for the voice, in order that the House of God may appear and may be in truth, the House of Prayer. (Session XXII: September 22, 1562: Decree regarding the things to be done or to be avoided during the celebration of Holy Mass.)

2. In order to improve the education and ecclesiastical formation of students in the Seminaries, these students must receive the tonsure and wear the clerical habit; to their other studies they must add the study of literature, *the Chant*, the computation of the ecclesiastical year, and the fine arts. (Session XXIII: July 15, 1563: Chapter 18: *Reform*).

---

[1] *Papal Documents on Sacred Music*, compiled by the Rt. Rev. Abbot Paul M. Ferretti, O.S.B. (New York: Society of St. Gregory of America, 1939), pp. 3-4. Reprinted by permission of *Sacred Music*, Journal of The Church Music Association of America.

3. All Canons are obliged to say the divine Office personally and not through a substitute; to assist the Bishop when he celebrates and pontificates; and to sing the praises of God in hymns and psalms in the Choir which has been organized for this purpose, and to do so with clearness and devotion. (Session XXIV: November 11, 1563: Chapter 12: *Reform*).

4. All other matters which concern the divine Office, the proper way of singing, the reunion of choirs and their right order and discipline . . . will be settled by the provincial Synod, which will prescribe for each province regulations which meet local needs and customs. For the moment, the Bishop assisted by at least two Canons, one of whom will be named by the Bishop and the other by the Chapter, will make the necessary decisions on matters that are most urgent. (From the same as above.)

Thomas Morley

(1557-1603)

Probably the most important musician of the Elizabethan period, Morley could easily have rested on the reputation of his delightful secular music. In addition, however, he wrote for the Church—Services, anthems, and psalm settings—and produced the valuable book of instruction, written in dialogue form, from which the present extract is taken. The text that immediately follows the excerpt about motets is printed in Oliver Strunk's anthology. [1] In it one can compare Morley's discussion of the secular music of his time with what he has said about motets.

Extract from A Plaine and Easie Introduction to Practicall Musicke [2]

A Motet is properlie a song made for the church, either vpon some hymne or Antheme, or such like, and that name I take to haue been giuen to that kinde of musicke in opposition to the other which they called *Canto fermo,* and we do commonlie call plainsong, for as nothing is more opposit to standing and firmness then motion, so did they giue the Motet that name of mouing, because it is in a manner quight contrarie to the other, which after some sort, and in respect of the other standeth still. [3] This kind of al others which are made on a ditty, requireth most art, and moueth and causeth most strange effects in the hearer, being aptlie framed for the dittie and well expressed by the singer, for it will draw the auditor (and speciallie the skilfull auditor) into a

---

[1]Oliver Strunk, *Source Readings in Music History* (New York: W. W. Norton & Company, Inc., 1950), pp. 274-78.

[2]Source: Thomas Morley, *A Plaine and Easie Introdvction to Practicall Mvsicke* (London: Peter Short, 1597), p. 179. Reprinted as No. 14 of *Shakespeare Association Facsimiles* (Oxford: Oxford University Press, 1937). Edition with modern spelling and punctuation, edited by R. Alec Harman (New York: W. W. Norton & Company, [1953?]).

[3]This comparison, which is inaccurate, seems to be Morley's own idea, and not one that was current in his time.

deuout and reuerent kind of consideration of him for whose praise
it was made. But I see not what passions or motions it can stirre
vp, being sung as most men doe commonlie sing it: that is,
leauing out the dittie and singing onely the bare note, as it were a
musicke made onelie for instruments, which will in deed shew the
nature of the musicke, but neuer carrie the spirit and (as it were)
that liuelie soule which the dittie giueth, but of this enough. And
to returne to the expressing of the ditty, the matter is now come
to that state that though a song be neuer so wel made & neuer so
aptlie applied to the words, yet shal you hardlie find singers to
expresse it as it ought to be, for most of our church men, (so they
can crie louder in ye quier then their fellowes) care for no more,
whereas by the contrarie, they ought to studie howe to vowell and
sing cleane, expressing their words with deuotion and passion,
whereby to draw the hearer as it were in chaines of gold by the
eares to the consideration of holie things. But this for the most
part, you shall find amongst them, that let them continue neuer so
long in the church, yea though it were twentie yeares, they will
neuer studie to sing better then they did the first day of their
preferment to that place, so that it should seeme that hauing
obtained the liuing which they sought for, they haue little or no
care at all either of their owne credit, or well discharging of that
dutie whereby they haue their maintenance. But to returne to our
Motets, if you compose in this kind, you must cause your
harmonie to carrie a maiestie taking discordes and bindings so
often as you canne, but let it be in long notes, for the nature of it
will not beare short notes and quick motions, which denotate a
kind of wantonnes.

This musicke (a lamentable case) being the chiefest both for art
and vtilitie, is notwithstanding little esteemed, and in small
request with the greatest number of those who most highly seeme
to fauor art, which is the cause that the composers of musick who
otherwise would follow the depth of their skill, in this kinde are
compelled for lacke of *maecenates* to put on another humor, and
follow that kind wherunto they haue neither beene brought vp,
nor yet (except so much as they can learne by seeing other mens
works in an vnknown tounge) doe perfectlie vnderstand ye nature
of it, such be the newfangled opinions of our countrey men, who
will highlie esteeme whatsoeuer commeth from beyond the seas,
and speciallie from Italie, be it neuer so simple, contemning that
which is done at home though it be neuer so excellent. Nor yet is
that fault of esteeming so highlie the light musicke particular to
vs in England, but generall through the world, which is the cause

that the musitions in all countries and chiefely in Italy, have imploied most of their studies in it: whereupon a learned man of our time writing vpon *Cicero* his dreame of *Scipio* saith, that the musicians of this age, in steed of drawing the minds of men to the consideration of heauen and heauenlie thinges, doe by the contrarie set wide open the gates of hell, causing such as delight in the exercise of their art tumble headlong into perdition.

THE SEVENTEENTH CENTURY

The Old Cheque-Book

(February 1, 1604)

The Old Cheque-Book of the Chapel Royal is a manuscript record of the activities carried on as part of the daily business of that famous center of British musical life. It contains documents concerning appointments, rules, penalties, memorable observances, and procedures between 1561 and 1744. Even in this best-staffed and most highly regarded of all English choral organizations there were problems. The orders issued at various times concerning the attendance of the adult members (see also pp.38-41*infra*) show only one side of the problem of staffing and maintaining such a choir.

Orders for the Attendance of the Gentlemen of his Majestes Chappell[1]

1. Every yeare within the twelve dayes of Christmas a list or rowle to be made new and drawne by the Subdeane and three or more of the gentlemen, to be chosen by the major parts of the fellowshipp in a Chapter called for that purpose, which gentlemen with the Subdeane shall then also dispose of their wayting in the Chappell by a monethly course, that a competent number of the gentlemen be appointed to attend the service upon the workinge dayes throughout the yeare (except in the accustomed tymes and weekes of libertye called playing weekes) under the penalty of a check for every one absence from any in his appointed monethe.

2. Uppon Sondayes, Principall tymes at Christmas, Easter, and Whitsontide, uppon holy dayes at bothe services, uppon festivall and offerynge daye eves, at evening prayer, uppon sermon dayes at morning prayers, all that shalbe in the aforsayd list and rowle of daylie wayters, aswell out of their appoynted moneth as in it, shall attend the service under penalty of a check for every absence.

---

[1]Source: Edward F. Rimbault, ed., *The Old Cheque-Book or Book of Remembrance of the Chapel Royal from 1561 to 1744*. ([London]: Printed for the Camden Society, 1872), pp. 71-73. Reprinted, New York: Da Capo Press, 1966.

3. If any of the gentlemen chaunce to be sicke or infirme, not able therby to attend in any parte of his wayting moneth, one of the juniors of a contrary moneth shalbe called by the appointment of the Subdeane to supply the tyme of his absence under payne of check for faylinge any service.

4. If any of the gentlemen in his appointed moneth shall have any urgent busines or any impediment to be approved by the Subdeane, his absence shalbe tollerated, provided that he procure another of the gentlemen of a contrary moneth and of his parte to wayte for him, and that the partye undertakinge such supply if he be defective therein he shalbe subject to check as in his owne moneth.

5. Every of the gentlemen called to wayte uppon any occasion by the Subdeane, though out of his waytynge moneth, shall obey and attend under paine of a check.

6. If any of the gentlemen shall departe out of the chappell in service tyme without leave of the Subdeane, and returne no more that service, he shall incurr the penalty of check of absence from all service.

7. It shalbe lawfull for the Subdeane, for the ease of any of the auntientier seniors, at his discrecon, to call the yonger juniors to wayte some parte of such senior's moneth, and they shall obey and performe the same under payne of a check.

8. If ther be above two Organistes at once, two shall allwaies attend; if ther be but two in all, then they shall wayte by course, one after an other, weekly or monethly, as they shall agree betwixt them selves, givinge notice to the Subdeane and the Clark of the Check how they do dispose of their waytinge, that therby it may be knowne who is at all tymes to be expected for the service, and they shalbe subject to such orders, and to such checks, in the same manner as the other gentlemen are.

9. The check for absence from morning prayers, holy dayes, festivall tymes, and sermon dayes, shalbe 4^d, from evening prayer uppon such dayes and their festivall eves 3^d, for absence from morninge prayer uppon workynge dayes 3^d, from eveninge prayer 2^d.

10. The check for late cominge, viz. after the first gloria patri 1^d, after the first lesson 2^d, after the second as for absent from the whole service.

11. If any shalbe over negligent, presuming that the ordinarie check shall excuse him from further penalty, he shalbe subject to such further check as the Subdeane shall thinke fitt to laye upon him.

12. All the checks shall monethly be divided amongst those of the gentlemen that have bin most diligent in wayting that moneth, by the judgment of the Subdeane of the moneth's wayters.

13. If any scruple or doubt arise concerning any point in these orders, it shalbe referred to the resolucon of the Deane of the Chappell, whose judgment shalbe theruppon obeyed.

The Old Cheque-Book

(February 2, 1625)

The description of the coronation ceremony of Charles I consists of instructions to the choir, enclosed by a few paragraphs that describe the decorations in Westminster Abbey. The service has much in common with other English coronation ceremonies, inasmuch as it is a religious ritual. Some of the same texts, therefore, are found in anthems of later composers, among them Purcell and Handel.

It is questionable whether the music at such a celebration was heard by many of those who gathered for the occasion. It is not possible to project the circumstances surrounding the coronation of Charles II backward to the event described here. Still, it is interesting to know that at the latter event, Samuel Pepys, who was able to have a seat on a scaffold at the north end of the Abbey, said that he could see only a portion of what went on, "but so great a noise that I could make but little of the musique; and indeed, it was lost to every body."[1]

The Order of the Chappell's service at the Coronaĉon of our Soveraigne Lord Kinge Charles, uppon Candlemas Day, in the first year of his raigne, Anno Domini 1625.[2]

Upon which day all the Chappell mett at the Colledge Hall in Westminster, wher they had a breakfast at the charge of the Colledge, from thence they went by a back way into the Church, and so into the vestrie, where together with the Quier of Westminster they putt on surplesses and copes and went into Westminster Hall, and there wayted until the Kinge came thither, who came from Whitehall by water, and landinge at the Parliament stayres came into the Great Hall, wher was a large scaffold covered all with cloth, and uppon it a throne and chayer

---

[1] *The Diary of Samuel Pepys*, ed. Henry B. Wheatley (2 vols.; New York: Random House, n.d.), I, 262.
[2] Source: Rimbault, ed., *The Old Cheque-Book*, pp. 157-60.

21

of estate, wher the Kinge sate untill the whole trayne weare marshaled in their order. The Chappell followed the Knights of the Privie Counsell, who went next after the Knights of the Bath, the Sergeant Porter with his black staff and Sergeant of the Vestry with his virger goinge before them; next the Quier of Westminster, then the Chappell, who went singinge through the Pallace yard and round about the Church, through the great Sanctuarie till they came to the west dore of the Church: when all the Chappell were within the Church they began the first Anthem.

> *I was glad when they sayd unto me we will goe into the house of the Lord, for thither the tribes goe up, even the tribes of the Lord, to testifie unto Israell, to give thankes unto the name of the Lord. For there is the seate of judgment, even the seate of the House of David. O pray for the peace of Jerusalem: they shall prosper that love thee.*

After the Archbishop hath don at the corners of the scaffold, and the people's acclamacõn ended, the Quire singeth

> *Strengthened be thy hand, and exalted be thy right hand. Righteousness and Peace be the preparacõn of thy seate, mercy and judgment ever goe before thy face. Allelujah: my songe shalbe alwaies of the lovinge kindnes of the Lord. Glory be to the Father, &c.*

When the sermon is ended, and after the Kinges Othe is taken, the Archbishop beginninge Come Holy Ghost, the Quire singeth

> *Come Holy Ghost, eternall God, proceeding from above,*
> *Both from the Father and the Sonne, the God of peace and love,*
> *Visitt our mindes, and into us the heavenly grace inspire,*
> *That in all truth and Godliness we may have true desire.*
> *Thou art the very Comforter in all woe and distresse,*
> *The heavenly guiftes of God most high, which no tong can expresse,*
> *The Fountain and the lyvely Spring of joy celestiall,*
> *The fire so bright, the love so cleare, and unction spirituall.*

After a prayer is read by the Archbishop, two other Bushops singe the Litany. And the Quire singethe the Answeres.

Whiles the Archbushop is annoyntinge the Kinge, the Quier singeth

Sadock the priest and Nathan the Prophett annoynted Salamon Kinge, and joyfully approchinge they cryed. God save the Kinge, God save the Kinge, God save the Kinge, for ever and ever. The Kinge shall rejoyce in thy strength, O Lord. Allelujah.

When the Crowne is sett uppon the Kinges head and the Archbushop hath ended the exhortation: Be strong and of a good courage, &c., the Quier singeth

The Kinge shall rejoyce in thy strength, O Lord, exceeding glad shall he be of thy salvation: for thou hast given him his hartes desire and hast not denied him the request of his lipps. Thou hast prevented him with the blessinges of goodnes, and hast sett a crowne of pure gould uppon his head. Allelujah.

When the Kinge hath done at the Alter, and is goinge to his Throne, the Quier singeth the Te Deum.

After the homage is done to the Kinge by the Lordes, and the Archbushop goeth to begin the Comunion, the Quier singeth

Behould, O God our Defendor, and looke uppon the face of thine Annointed, for one day in thy Courtes is better then a thousand. O how amiable are thy tabernacles, thou Lord of Hostes. Allelujah.

Then followeth the Comunion, and when the Epistle and Gospell are ended, being read by the Bushops, the Quier singeth the Nicene Creed, the Archbushop beginning yt.

After the Offitorie vearse is read by the Archbishop, the Offitorie beginneth with this Anthem, beinge songe by the Quier:

Lett my prayer be sett forth in thy presence like unto the incense. Lett the liftinge up of my handes be as an evening sacrifice. Allelujah.

After this then is ended, the organs playe till the Offitorie be ended. Then the holies and the Et in terra pax, &c., as in the Comunion book, to be songe by the Quier, except the Archbushop will read them. After the Comunion is finished, the Quier singeth

O hearken then unto the voyce of my callinge, my Kinge and my God, for unto Thee will I make my prayer.

Then the ordinarie collects in the Comon Prayer Booke after the Comunion beinge read by the Archbushop, and the prayer of God, &c., so all is ended.

After all the ceremonie in the Church was ended, the Kinge returned back againe into Westminster Hall in the same manner as he went, the Chappell goeinge in their former order, and singinge all the waye till they came to Westminster Hall dore, and their they stayed, makinge a lane for the Kinge and all the Lordes to passe betwixt them, and continued singinge till the Kinge was within the Hall: and from thence they returned back into the Church, where in the vestry they putt of their copes and surplusses, and came to White hall, wher they had some allowance of diett for they suppers.

All the way from the scaffold in the Great Hall, through the Pallace yard and the street in the Great Sanctuarie, unto the scaffold in the Quier of the Church, was strowed with russhes and uppon the russhes covered with blew broad cloth.

Thomas Ravenscroft

(ca.1590-ca.1633)

By the time Ravenscroft's psalter appeared in 1621, the greater part of a century of psalter publication had elapsed. Anyone entering the now competitive field needed more than simply another collection of metrical psalms with tunes or four-part settings. Ravenscroft's volume was large — the only one containing more pieces was that of John Day, published in 1563 — and many of the harmonizations were his own. Probably his reputation as a composer helped greatly in the sale of the volume, for he had produced a number of popular collections of secular music earlier in the century. In addition, he was able to advertise that composers of the other tunes in the collection included Thomas Tallis, John Dowland, Thomas Morley, Thomas Tomkins, and sixteen other important men of that and the preceding generations. That most of these composers had been represented in earlier psalters is true, but there were ten new names in the list, including Ravenscroft himself who supplied more than fifty harmonizations.

There are two introductory sections to the volume: an opening explanation dedicated "to all that have skill, or will vnto sacred musicke," and the apologia printed here. It is evident that the furor over when psalms were to be sung, or whether they were to be sung by the entire congregation, was not an issue at this time, although the matter was to be discussed at great length by John Cotton and numerous other American writers.

Of the Praise, Vertue, and Efficacie of the Psalmes.[1]

The *Kingly Prophet David*, Psal. 47. 6. saith; O sing praises, sing praises vnto our God, O sing praises, sing praises vnto our King: Sing praises with vnderstanding. Againe, Psal. 95. 2. Let vs shew our selues glad in him with Psalmes. And good reason haue we to sing chearefully vnto God, for the Angels ioyne their presence & congratulation with the singers deuotion, as the same Psalmist singeth, Psal. 138. *In conspectu angelorum psallam tibi*; Euen before

---

[1]Source: Thomas Ravenscroft, *The Whole Booke of Psalmes* (2nd ed.; London: Thomas Harper, 1633), pp. xv-xvi.

the Gods will I sing praise vnto thee: Wherefore we ought diligently to take heed, that by our idlenesse, negligence, and want of practise, wee cause not the *Angels* to depart from vs. And indeed there is no mortall man which can expresse in words, or conceiue in thought, the vertues of the Psalmes, and the praises of the Lord, if with a pure and serious attention of the heart they shall be performed as they ought to be.

In the Psalmes, are described the rewards of good, the punishments of euil men, the rudiments of beginners, the progresse of proficients, and consummation of perfect men.

The singing of Psalmes (as say the Doctors) comforteth the sorrowfull, pacifieth the angry, strengtheneth the weake, humbleth the proud, gladdeth the humble, stirres vp the flow, reconcileth enemies, lifteth vp the heart to heauenly things, and vniteth the Creature to his Creator, for whatsoeuer is in the Psalmes, conduceth to the edification, benefit, and consolation of mankinde.

Wouldst thou make a confession, and repent thee of thy sinnes? Then sing with remorse and humility the seauen penitential Psalms of *David,* and thou shalt feele the sweet mercy of God and thy minde refreshed with spirituall joy.

Wouldst thou pray? Then poure forth thy soule in the Psalmes 25. 54. 67. 70. 72. 86. 143. For the soule of man cannot either feelingly expresse his misery, tribulation and anguish of temptation, or more powerfully call vpon the mercy of God, then in these Psalmes.

Wouldst thou praise the Maiestie of God, or giue him thankes for all his benefits? then sing the 103, 104, 105, 106, 107, 108, 111, 113, 144, 145, 146, 147, 148, 149, 150.

If thou be so farre afflicted with outward and inward temptations, that thou seemest to be forsaken, then sing heartily the 22. 64. 69. Psalmes.

If this present life be tedious vnto thee, and that with an ardent desire thou waitest to see God, then sing the 42, 63, 84. Psalmes.

If thou finde thy selfe quite deiected, and as it were forlorne in trouble, then with compunction of heart sing the 13, 31, 44, 54, 56. Psalmes, and when thou hast found ease and rest vnto thy soule, O sing to the praise of God, the 30, 34, 103, 104. Psalmes, and always whether in the time of aduersity, or prosperity, sing out the song of the three Children, wherein euery creature is inuited to praise God.

But dost thou desire to exercise thy selfe in the diuine praises and precepts of the Lord? Content thy selfe then and sing the 119. Psalme, wherein although euen to the end of thy life thou shalt haue sought and searcht all that thou canst, yet shalt thou neuer perfectly vnderstand the vertues & excellencies, or reach vnto the heights and depths which are comprehended in it: for hardly is there a verse in that whole Psalme wherein is not mention made of Gods Law, Commandments, Testimonies and Precepts.

In a word, he that would giue these heauenly Hymnes their due, had need to compose a Psalme in praise of the Psalmes, that so the deuout and joyfull soule might with looking vp vnto God, reflect vpon its own worke, and transport it selfe vnto the quire of Angels and Saints, whose perpetuall taske is to sing their concording parts without pause, redoubling and descanting; *Holy, Holy, Holy, Lord God of Hosts.* And if Vocall Musicke be not full enough, let the Instrumentall be added, *Reuelat.* 15. 2. They haue in their hands the Harps of God & sing the song of *Moses,* and the song of the Lambe, saying, *Great and marvaiieus* [marvellous] *are thy works Lord God Almighty.* Amen.

The Bay Psalm Book

(1640)

The first printed books in the New World appeared in Mexico City before the middle of the sixteenth century. Among them were a number of works that contained music. They have often been passed over because of the great emphasis that is laid upon The Bay Psalm Book, a work that contained no music in its early editions, and that came into print fully a century later than the first printed work in the Catholic settlements. This later arrival on the scene remained in use for a long time, appearing in numerous editions over the next century, with music after 1690. Often mentioned nowadays, but rarely examined, The Bay Psalm Book was the result of the Puritan colony's wanting a book different from that used by the Pilgrim settlers, for the latter were Separatists and the Puritans wanted no identification with that degree of rebellion.

The Preface to the book, probably written by John Cotton, sets out in clear, but sometimes repetitious, detail a justification for the new poetic settings made for this volume by a sizable group of the founding fathers and immigrants. While it seems strange that a large part of the Preface is given over to the debate about congregational singing versus worship *in petto*, it is no less amazing that the battle over singing still raged a century later, when the supporters of "regular singing" aligned themselves against the old-fashioned followers of the "lining-out" method.

The Preface.[1]

The singing of Psalmes, though it breath forth nothing but holy harmony, and melody: yet such is the subtilty of the enemie, and the enmity of our nature against the Lord, & his wayes, that our hearts can finde matter of discord in this harmony, and crotchets of division in this holy melody.-for- There have been

---

[1]Source: *The Whole Booke of Psalmes Faithfully Translated into English Metre* ([Cambridge, Mass.: Stephen Daye], 1640). Reprinted in facsimile, New York: Dodd, Mead, and Company, 1903; Chicago: The University of Chicago Press, 1956.

three questiõs especially stirrĩg cõcerning singing. First. what psalmes are to be sung in churches? whether Davids and other scripture psalmes, or the psalmes invented by the gifts of godly men in every age of the church. Secondly, if scripture psalmes, whether in their owne words, or in such meter as english poetry is wont to run in? Thirdly. by whom are they to be sung? whether by the whole churches together with their voices? or by one man alõe and the rest joynĩg in silẽce, & in the close sayĩg amen.

Touching the first, certainly the singing of Davids psalmes was an acceptable worship of God, not only in his owne, but in succeeding times. as in Solomons time *2 Chron.*5.13. in Iehosaphats time *2 chron.*20.21. in Ezra his time *Ezra* 3.10,11. and the text is evident in Hezekiahs time they are commanded to sing praise in the words of David and Asaph, *2 chron.* 29,30. which one place may serve to resolve two of the questions (the first and the last) at once. for this commandement was it cerimoniall or morall? some things in it indeed were cerimoniall, as their musicall instruments &c but what cerimony was there in singing prayse with the words of David and Asaph? what if David was a type of Christ, was Asaph also? was every thing of David typicall? are his words (which are of morall, universall, and perpetuall authority in all nations and ages) are they typicall? what type can be imagined in making use of his songs to prayse the Lord? If they were typicall because the cerimony of musicall instruments was joyned with them, then their prayers were also typicall, because they had that ceremony of incense admixt with them: but wee know that prayer then was a morall duty, notwithstanding the incense; and soe singing those psalmes notwithstanding their musicall instruments. Beside, that which was typicall (as that they were sung with musicall instruments, by the twenty-foure orders of Priests and Levites. *1 chron* 25.9.) must have the morall and spirituall accomplishment in the new Testament, in all the Churches of the Saints principally, who are made kings & priests *Rev.*1.6. and are the first fruits unto God. *Rev.* 14. 4. as the Levites were *Num.*3.45. with hearts & lippes, in stead of musicall instruments, to prayse the Lord; who are set forth (as some iudiciously thinke) *Rev.*4.4. by twẽty foure Elders, in the ripe age of the Church, *Gal.*4.1,2,3. answering to the twenty foure orders of Priests and Levites 1 chron. 25. 9. Therefore not some select members, but the whole Church is commaunded to teach one another in all the severall sorts of Davids psalmes, some being called by himselfe מזמורים : psalms, some תהלים : Hymns some שירים :spirituall songs. soe that if the singing Davids

psalmes be a morall duty & therfore perpetuall; then wee under
the new Testamēt are bound to sing them as well as they under
the old: and if wee are expresly commanded to sing Psalmes,
Hymnes, and spirituall songs, then either we must sing Davids
psalmes, or else may affirm they are not spirituall songs: which
being penned by an extraordīary gift of the Spirit, for the sake
especially of Gods spirtuall Israell; not to be read and preached
only (as other parts of holy writ) but to be sung also, they are
therefore most spirituall, and still to be sung of all the Israell of
God: and verily as their sin is exceeding great, who will allow
Davids psalmes (as other scriptures) to be read in churches (which
is one end) but not to be preached also, (which is another end soe
their sin is crying before God, who will allow them to be read and
preached, but seeke to deprive the Lord of the glory of the third
end of them, which is to sing them in christian churches.

obj. 1 If it be sayd that the Saints in the primitive Church did
compile spirituall songs of their owne inditing, and sing them
before the Church. 1 Cor. 14, 15, 16.

Ans. We answer first, that those Saints compiled these spirituall
songs by the extraordinary gifts of the spirit (common in those
dayes) whereby they were inabled to praise the Lord in strange
tongues, wherin learned *Paraus* proves those psalmes were uttered,
in his Commēt on that place *vers* 14 which extraordinary gifts, if
thy were still in the Churches, wee should allow them the like
liberty now. Secondly, suppose those psalmes were sung by an
ordinary gift (which wee suppose cannot be evicted) doth it
therefore follow that they did not, & that we ought not to sing
Davids psalmes? must the ordinary gifts of a private man quench
the spirit still speaking to us by the extraordinary gifts of his
servant David? there is not the least foot-step of example, or
precept, or colour reason for such a bold practice.

obj. 2. Ministers are allowed to pray conceived prayers, and why
not to sing conceived psalmes: must wee not sing in the spirit as
well as pray in the spirit?

Ans. First because every good minister hath not a gift of
spirituall poetry to compose extemporary psalmes as he hath of
prayer. Secondly. Suppose he had, yet seeing psalmes are to be
sung by a joynt consent and harmony of all the Church in heart
and voyce (as wee shall prove) this cannot be done except he that
composeth a psalme, bringeth into the Church set formes of
psalmes of his owne invētion; for which wee finde no warrant or
president in any ordinary officers of the Church throughout the
sciptures. Thirdly. Because the booke of psalmes is so compleat a

System of psalmes, which the Holy-Ghost himselfe in infinite wisdome hath made to suit all the conditions, necessityes, temptations, affections, &c. of men in all ages; (as most of all our interpreters on the psalmes have fully and perticularly cleared) therefore by this the Lord seemeth to stoppe all mens mouths and mindes ordinarily to compile or sing any other psalmes (under colour that the ocasions and conditions of the Church are new) &c. for the publick use of the Church, seing, let our condition be what it will, the Lord himselfe hath supplyed us with farre better; and therefore in Hezekiahs time, though doubtlesse there were among them those which had extraordinary gifts to compile new songs on those new ocasions, as Isaiah and Mica &c. yet wee read that they are commanded to sing in the words of David and Asaph, which were ordinarily to be used in the publick worship of God: and wee doubt not but those that are wise will easily see; that those set formes of psalmes of Gods owne appoyntment not of mans conceived gift or humane imposition were sung in the Spirit by those holy Levites, as well as their prayers were in the spirit which themselves conceived, the Lord not then binding them therin to any set formes; and shall set formes of psalmes appoynted of God not be sung in the spirit now, which others did then? Question. But why may not one cōpose a psalme and sing it alone with a loud voice & the rest joyne with him in silence and in the end say Amen?

Ans. If such a practise was found in the Church of Corinth, when any had a psalme suggested by an extraordinary gift; yet in singing ordinary psalmes the whole Church is to ioyne together in heart and voyce to prayse the Lord. -for-
First. Davids psalmes as hath beene shewed, were sung in heart and voyce together by the twenty foure orders of the musicians of the Temple, who typed out the twenty foure Elders all the members especially of christian Churches *Rev* 5.8. who are made Kings and Priests to God to prayse him as they did: for if there were any other order of singing Choristers beside the body of the people to succeed those, the Lord would doubtlesse have given direction in the gospell for their quallification, election, maintainance &c. as he did for the musicians of the Temple, and as his faithfullnes hath done for all other church officers in the new Testament.
Secondly. Others beside the Levites (the chiefe Singers) in the Jewish Church did also sing the Lords songs; else why are they commanded frequently to sing: as in ps.100, 1,2,3. ps.95, 1,2,3. ps.102. title. with vers 18. & *Ex*.15.1. not only Moses but all

Israell sang that song, they spake saying (as it is in the *orig.*) all as
well as Moses, the women also as well as the men. v.20 21. and
*deut.*32. (whereto some thinke, Iohn had reference as well as to
*Ex.*15.1. when he brings in the protestant Churches getting the
victory over the Beast with harps in their hands and singing the
song of Moses *Rev.*15. 3.) this song Moses is commanded not only
to put it into their hearts but into their mouths also: *deut.*31. 19.
which argues, they were with their mouths to sing it together as
well as with their hearts.

Thirdly. Isaiah foretells in the dayes of the new-Testament that
Gods watchmen and desolate lost soules, (signified by wast places)
should with their voices sing together, Isa.52. 8,9. and *Rev.*7. 9,10.
the song of the Lamb was by many together, and the Apostle
expresly commands the singing of Psalmes, Himnes, &c. not to
any select christians, but to the whole Church Eph. 5. 19 *coll.*3.
16. Paule & Silas sang together in private *Acts.*16. 25. and must
the publick heare ōly one man sing? to all these wee may adde the
practise of the primitive Churches; the testimony of ancient and
holy *Basil* is in stead of many *Epist.* 63 When one of us (saith he)
hath begun a psalme, the rest of us set in to sing with him, all of
us with one heart and one voyce; and this saith he is the common
practise of the Churches in Egypt, Lybia, Thebes, Palstina, Syria
and those that dwell on Euphrates, and generally every where,
where singing of psalmes is of any account. To the same purpose
also *Eusebius* give witnes, *Eccles. Hist. lib.* 2. *cap.* 17. The objections
made against this doe most of them plead against joyning to sing
in heart as well as in voyce, as that by this meanes others out of
the Church will sing as also that wee are not alway in a sutable
estate to the matter sung, & likewise that all cannot sing with
understanding; shall not therefore all that have understanding
ioyne in heart and voyce together? are not all the creatures in
heaven, earth, seas: men, beasts, fishes, soules &c. commanded to
praise the Lord, and yet none of these but men, and godly men
too, can doe it with spirituall understanding?

As for the scruple that some take at the translatiō of the book
of psalmes into meeter, because Davids psalmes were sung in his
owne words without meeter: wee answer- First. There are many
verses together in several psalmes of David which run in rithmes
(as those that know the hebrew and as Buxtorf shews *Thesau.* pa.
629.) which shews at least the lawfullnes of singing psalmes in
english rithmes.

Secondly. The psalmes are penned in such verses as are sutable
to the poetry of the hebrew language, and not in the common

style of such other bookes of the old Testament as are not
poeticall; now no protestant doubteth but that all the bookes of
the scripture should by Gods ordinance be extant in the mother
tongue of each nation, that they may be understood of all, hence
the psalmes are to be translated into our english tongue; and if in
our english tongue wee are to sing them, then as all our english
songs (according to the course of our english poetry) do run in
metre, soe ought Davids psalmes to be translated into meeter, that
soe wee may sing the Lords songs, as in our english tongue soe in
such verses as are familar to an english eare which are commonly
metricall: and as it can be no just offence to any good conscience
to sing Davids hebrew songs in english words, soe neither to sing
his poeticall verses in english poeticall metre: men might as well
stumble at singing the hebrew psalmes in our english tunes (and
not in the hebrew tunes) as at singing them in english meeter,
(which are our verses) and not in such verses as are generally used
by David according to the poetry of the hebrew language: but the
truth is, as the Lord hath hid from us the hebrew tunes, lest we
should think our selves bound to imitate them; soe also the course
and frame (for the most part) of their hebrew poetry, that wee
might not think our selves bound to imitate that, but that every
nation without scruple might follow as the graver sort of tunes of
their owne country songs, soe the graver sort of verses of their
owne country poetry.

Neither let any think, that for the meetre sake wee have taken
liberty or poeticall licence to depart from the true and proper
sence of Davids words in the hebrew verses, noe; but it hath beene
one part of our religious care and faithfull indeavour, to keep close
to the originall text.

As for the obiections taken from the difficulty of *Ainsworths*
tunes, and the corruptions in our common psalme books, wee hope
they are answered in this new edition of psalmes which wee here
present to God and his Churches. For although wee have cause to
blesse God in many respects for the religious indeavours of the
translaters of the psalmes into meetre usually annexed to our
Bibles, yet it is not unknowne to the godly learned that they have
rather presented a paraphrase then the words of David translated
according to the rule 2 *chron*. 29. 30. and that their addition to
the words, detractions from the words are not seldome and rare,
but very frequent and many times needles, (which we suppose
would not be approved of if the psalmes were so translated into
prose) and that their variations of the sense, and alterations of the
sacred text too frequently, may iustly minister matter of offence to

them that are able to compare the translation with the text; of which failings, some iudicious have oft complained, others have been grieved, wherupon it hath bin generally desired, that as wee doe inioye this ordinance also in its native purity: wee have therefore done our indeavour to make a plaine and familiar translation of the psalmes and words of David into english metre, and have not soe much as presumed to paraphrase to give the sense of his meaning in other words; we have therefore attended heerin as our chief guide the originall, shūning all additions, except such as even the best translators of them in prose supply, avoiding all materiall detractions from word or sence. The word ו which we translate *and* as it is redundant sometime in the Hebrew, soe somtime (though not very often) it hath been left out, and yet not then, if the sence were not faire without it.

As for our translations, wee have with our english Bibles (to which next to the Originall wee have had respect) used the Idioms of our owne tongue in stead of Hebraismes, lest they might seeme english barbarismes. Synonimaes wee use indifferently: as *folk* for *people,* and *Lord* for *Iehovah,* and somtime (though seldome) *God* for *Iehovah;* for which (as for some other interpretations of places cited in the new Testament) we have the scriptures authority ps. 14 with 53. Heb. 1. 6. with psalme 97. 7. Where a phrase is doubtfull wee have followed that which (in our owne apprehensiō) is most genuine & edifying:

Somtime wee have contracted, somtime dilated the same hebrew word, both for the sence and the verse sake: which dilatation wee conceive to be no paraphrasticall addition no more then the contraction of a true and full translation to be any unfaithfull detraction or diminution: as when wee dilate *who healeth* and say *he it is who healeth:* soe when wee contract, *those that stand in awe of God* and say *Gods fearers.*

Lastly. Because some hebrew words have a more full and emphaticall signification then any one english word can or doth somtime expresse, hence wee have done that somtime which faithfull translators may doe, *viz.* not only to translate the word but the emphasis of it; as אל *mighty God.* for God. ברך *humbly blesse* for *blesse: rise to stand.* psalm 1. for *stand: truth and faithfullnes* for *truth.* Howbeit for the verse sake wee doe not alway thus, yet wee render the word truly though not fully; as when wee somtime say *reioyce* for *shout for ioye.*

As for all other changes of number, tenses, and characters of speech, they are such as either the hebrew will unforcedly beare, or our english forceably calls for, or they no way change the sence;

and such are printed usually in another character.

If therefore the verses are not alwayes so smooth and elegant as some may desire or expect; let them consider that Gods Altar needs not our pollishings: Ex. 20. for wee have respected rather a plaine translation, then to smooth our verses with the sweetnes of any paraphrase, and soe have attended Conscience rather then Elegance, fidelity rather then poetry, in translating the hebrew words into english language, and Davids poetry into english meetre; that soe wee may sing in Sion the Lords songs of prayse according to his owne will; untill hee takes us from hence, and wipe away all our teares, & bid us enter into our masters ioye to sing eternall Halleluiahs.

Edward Lowe

(ca.1610-1682)

Whatever else resulted from the interruption to cathedral practice during the Commonwealth, a matter of great concern was the almost total unemployment of church musicians. The substitution of psalm singing for the formal aspects of the previously acceptable Church of England required and welcomed no professional skills. When the Republican Interregnum ended with the return of Charles II, the immediate problem of filling choirs, parish and cathedral, with singers who could perform a cathedral-type Service was not easily solved. Many of the adult musicians of the previous decades had either gone into other work or were not survivors to the new era; no children had been trained to the treble parts for a dozen years. One of the few survivors,[1] Lowe published a short volume of simple four-part pieces intended to fill the gap while it trained musicians to the nearly lost traditions he knew. Few copies of his pamphlet survive. The music will not be missed, but his introduction deserves to be read as evidence of the problem he tried to solve.

To all Gentlemen that are true Lovers of Cathedrall Musicke.[2]

Gentlemen:

It is too well known that hath bin practised in Cathedrall Churches (in order to the publique worship of God, for many years past) instead of Harmony and Order. And therefore it may be rationally supposed, that the Persons and things relating to both, are not easily rallyed, after so fatall a Route. But Since the mercy of God hath restored a Power, and by it put life into the Law, to promote and settle it as it was. It hath been judged convenient, to

---

[1]The revival of cathedral tradition, and the part played by Lowe's contemporaries, is discussed in Chapter II of Elwyn A. Wienandt and Robert H. Young, *The Anthem in England and America* (New York: The Free Press, 1970).

[2]E[dward]. L[owe]. *A Short Direction for the Performance of Cathedrall Service* (Oxford: William Hall, 1661), p. 2.

revive the generall practice of the ordinary performance of Cathedrall service for the use of them, who shall be called to it, and are desirous to doe it with devotion and alacritie. To this end a Person is willingly imployed, who have been, understood, and bore a part in the same from his Childhood: And therein thinks himselfe happy to be now a Meane Instrument to doe God, and the Church service, in such a time when there are so many Cathedralls to be furnisht, and so few Persons knowing enough (in this particular) to performe the solemnity requisite in them: He hath therefore put together and published, The Ordinary and Extraordinary parts, both for the Priest, and whole Quire. Hoping that his Brethren in the same Imployment will look on it as Candidly as he intends it, since what is done, is only as a help to those that are Ignorant of it. The tunes in foure parts, to serve only so long, till the Quires are more learnedly Musicall, and thereby a greater variety used. Lastly 'tis fit some few reasons be given why, as directions how it may be understood in this form.

The Old Cheque-Book

(December 19, 1663)

The reorganization of the Chapel Royal after the Restoration posed a number of problems. Some of the Gentlemen of the Chapel had died or were otherwise unavailable after the lengthy interruption of liturgical activity by the period of Republican rule. Choristers were unavailable, of course, their training having been impossible. Charles II returned to England at the end of May, 1660, bringing an end to what John Evelyn called "a sad, & long Exile, and Calamitous Suffering both of the King & Church." [1] Shortly thereafter, Henry Cooke (C.1616-1672) was appointed to a position as "bass in the Chapel Royal and Master of the Children. It was not a cheerful prospect for a musician, for there were only five old members, no books, no surplices to wear, and the order of service so entirely forgotten that no two organists played it alike."[2] It was early in Cooke's tenure of office that the following rules were formulated. It is apparent that they were patterned after the orders issued in 1604 (*cf.* pp. 18-20 *supra*). That there are more of them, and those more specific than the earlier set, shows clearly the amount of reorganization that had to be undertaken.

At a Chapter holden in the Vestry at Whitehall by the Reverend Father in God George Lord Bishop of Winton for the better regulating of the Divine service in his Majesties Chappell Royall, the nineteenth day of December 1663, and in the fifteenth yeare of his Majesties reigne, it is thus ordered: —[3]

1. To the end that the great neglects in God's service may be redrest in his Majesties Chappell Royall it is required that the Subdeane take care that these orders be put in due execution.

[1] *The Diary of John Evelyn*, ed. E. S. de Beer (6 vols.; Oxford: At the Clarendon Press, 1955), III, 246.
[2] *Grove's Dictionary of Music and Musicians*, ed. Eric Blom (10 vols., 5th ed.; New York: St. Martin's Press, 1954-61), II, 420.
[3] Source: Rimbault, ed., *The Old Cheque-Book*, pp. 81-84.

2. All the gentlemen and officers and children shall yield obedience to the Deane and Subdeane and their Substitutes in all things touching the service to be performed in the Chappell: whosoever shall refuse shall undergoe such a check as they shall impose upon him.

3. No man shalbe admitted a Gentleman of his Majesties Chappell Royall but shall first quit all interest in other quires, and those that relate at present to other churches besides the Chappell, shall declare their choice either to fix at their churches, or to the Chappell, by the first day of March, his Majestie not permitting them to belong to both. And all the Gentlemen of his Majesties Chappell shall have their habitations within or neer the City of London, to be ready to attend at all times when the Deane or Sub Deane shall summon them.

4. Every gentleman and officer of the vestry shall give a note to the Sub Deane of the place of their aboad, that he may know where to send for them upon occasion.

5. The service shalbe appointed by the Deane or Sub Deane or his Substitute, with advice of the Master of the Children, for such Anthems as are to be performed by the Children of the Chappell.

6. The gentlemen being decently habited in their gownes and surplices (not in cloakes and bootes and spurrs) shall come into the Chappell orderly together, and attend God's service at the hours of ten and foure on the weeke dayes, and at nine and foure on Sundayes and Sermon dayes, and not depart till prayers are ended then to returne their surplices to the Standard.

7. All the Gentlemen in Generall being placed in their seates shall use their bookes and voyces in the Psalmodies and Responsalls according to the order of the Rubricke, and in the hymnes of the Church in the time of Divine service, and answer the Amen in a loud voice.

8. None of the Gentlemen shall plead priviledge above another for absence in his month of waiting, upon any occasion whatsoever, but if any one happen to be sicke, or have occasion of busines, to be approved by the Deane or Sub Deane, whereby he cannott attend the service, he shall procure one of his owne part, who is to waite in another month to supply his roome under paine of forfeiting a double check.

9. All the Gentlemen in General shall give their attendance at the service in his Majesties Chappell Royall on Sundayes and Holydayes and their eves; whosoever shall be absent shall forfeit a double checke.

10. The check for absence on ordinary weeke dayes shall be

twelve pence every service; on Sundayes, Holydayes and their eves two shillings a service.

11. Every Gentleman that shall come into the Chappell after the first Gloria Patri, shall be accounted tardy and be mulct sixpence; if he come after the first lesson, he shalbe accounted absent and pay the whole check.

12. Whosoever shall be over negligent, presuming the ordinary check shall excuse him, shalbe subject to such farther check as the Deane or Sub Deane shall lay upon him.

13. If the Subdeane shall see cause to require any gentleman to waite, though out of his month, the said gentleman shall obey and attend, under such a checke as the Subdeane with the Deanes consent shall lay upon him.

14. Every Gentleman sworne extraordinary shall waite constantly in his Majesties Chappell, till his place fall, and shall be approv'd of both for manners, skill, and voyce, before he be admitted.

15. Whosoever shall be admitted into a Priest's place in the Chappell shall sweare to take on him the office of a Deacon the next Ordinacōn and to doe the service thereunto belonging.

16. Of the three Organistes two shall ever attend, one at the organ, the other in his surplice in the quire, to beare a parte in the Psalmodie and service. At solemne times they shall all three attend. The auncientest organist shall serve and play the service on the eve and daye of the solemne feastes, viz: Christmas, Easter, St. George, and Whitsonside. The second organist shall serve the second day, and the third the third day. Other dayes they shall wait according to their monthes.

17. The Sub Deane shall take care that an impartiall bill of perdicōns for absence be duely kept and delivered to the Clerke of the Checke at the end of every quarter, to be defalkt out of the salaries of all who are negligent, or have uppon default been mulcted, the which said summe of mulctes shall be delivered by the Clerk of the Checke into the Sub Deanes hands with all dead pay, if any shall happen to be disposed off, as the Deane shall order and direct.

18. It is ordered upon his Majesties bountifull liberallitie in augmenting the salaries of the Gentlemen and others, that since the care and labour of the Clerke of the Checke is become greater then heretofore, he shall receive 2^d in the pound out of every Gentleman's salary or pension, as oft as he payes them.

19. The Sergeant, Yeomen, and Groome of the Vestry shall dayly attend the service in the Chappell at the hours of prayer; the Sergeant shall every day before prayers deliver the Gentlemen their

surplices out of the standard, and every Gentleman shall return his surplice to the standard when service is ended. The Sergeant of the Vestry shall not endeavour to procure any warrant, for standards or other necessary utensills for the service of the Chappell, except the old be first adjudged unserviceable under the hands of the Deane and Subdeane for the time being, and the utensills unserviceable shall be the fees of the Sergeant, except the King's Majestie command otherwise.

20. The Yeomen by turnes shall make ready the alter and take care that all the service and singing bookes and plate, with the surplices, be dayly returned to the standard, ibidem.

21. The officers of the Chappell shall take care that no persons be placed in the Gentlemen's seates without leave of the Deane or Subdeane.

GEOR. WINTON.

22. No man to take any booke out of the Chappell but he is to enter it into the Cheque Booke, or to leave a note with the Sergeant.

Decree on Sacred Music

(July 30, 1665)

The intrusion of secular features, in the form of solo singing, dramatic rearrangement of texts, additional musical numbers to serve as a sort of religious concert, and the growing prominence of the choirs themselves, may be seen in the following document. Important pronouncements on musical practice tend either to reflect some new practice or to prevent an impending challenge to tradition. The text that follows seems to have elements of both functions.

Decree on Sacred Music by the Sacra Visita Apostolica[1]
(July 30, 1665)

Resúme´

1. All music for use at Mass or divine Office, — psalms, antiphons, motets, hymns, chants, etc., — must be truly ecclesiastical in style, grave and devout in character.

2. After the Epistle the only thing that may be sung is the Gradual or the Tract; after the Credo, no other words but those of the Offertory; after the *Sanctus*. the *Benedictus*. or else a Motet, provided the words thereof are those which the Church uses in the Breviary or in the Missal in honor of the Blessed Sacrament.

3. At Vespers, the only thing that may be sung, apart from the psalms and the hymn, are the Antiphons of the feast of that day as prescribed by the Breviary. The same rule applies to Compline.

4. To sing with a solo voice, whether high or low, a hymn or a motet, in whole or in large part, is forbidden. But to vary the chant of the full chorus, the voices may be *alternated*. taking sometimes a group of equal voices, sometimes the low voices alone, sometimes the high voices.

---

[1] *Papal Documents on Sacred Music*, p. 4. Reprinted by permission of *Sacred Music*. Journal of The Church Music Association of America.

5. The words of the Breviary and of the Missal, as well as those taken from Holy Scripture and from the writings of the Fathers must be put to music exactly as they are, without inverting their order, without alteration of any kind, nor the insertion of extraneous words.

6. During Passiontide, it is forbidden to play the organ.

7. Rectors of Churches are given a period of twenty days in which to provide for the construction of fine grills to surround their choirs, whether these choirs be stationary or moveable, which grills must be high enough to hide the singers completely from view, and this, under pain of suspension from office.

Thomas Mace

(ca.1613-1709?)

Too often considered merely as a manual of performance practice, Mace's volume has had disproportionate attention given to his excellent discussion of instrumental music. The author was, nevertheless, a devout Anglican, concerned with the poor musical conditions that prevailed in parish and country churches. His solution to the problems he saw is visionary; his style may well be filled with hyperbole, but the problems he discusses have been common to many congregations, English and American.

Extracts from Musick's Monument [1]

I will now proceed and make good my Promise; and propose an *undoubted way* how the *Psalms* may be *exactly* performed, to the great *illustration* of the *Service of the Church. your own comforts.* and the *Glory of God: infinitely* beyond whatever has been, or can be by the contrary.

And because I have made it manifest how difficult a thing it is for any *person* to Sing in *Tune alone:* but *ten times more difficult* when he is within hearing of any *who sings out of Tune:* (nor is it possible for any to do it) It is to be noted, that where *Nature* is *deficient.* or *obstructed. God Almighty* has infus'd into the *Understandings* of men *wit and ingenuity.* by *Art* to be assisting unto *it.*

And it is known by all *experience.* that there are certain ways found out in *this Art* to cause men and women, who are but of *indifferent capacities.* (as to *Musick*) so to Sing in *Tune* that (at the worst) they shall not *interrupt* or *disturb* any who are within hearing of them, but (with a very little *use* and *practice*) they shall *assist and augment* the *Chorus* to very *good purpose.*

[1]Source: Thomas Mace, *Musick's Monument* . . . (London: For the author, 1676), pp. 8-9, 10-11, 15, 22-25. Reprint, Paris: Editions du centre national de la recherche scientifique, 1958.

Chap. V.

Now as to this, there is no *better way* to Sing to some *certain Instrument*, nor is there any *Instrument* so *proper* for a *Church* as an *Organ*; so that it will follow by right *reason* in *consequence*, that if you will *Sing Psalms* in *Churches well*, and in *Tune*, *you must needs have an Organ* to Sing unto; by which means the *whole Congregation* will be drawn (or as it were *compell'd*) into *Harmonical unity*: even so, that 'tis *impossible* for any person, who has but a *common or indifferent Ear*, (as most people have) to Sing *out of Tune*.

This is the way, and *None* in *compare* unto it; nor can the performance be *excellent without it*, or as it ought to be.

For when we Sing unto *God*, we ought to Sing *chearfully*, and with a *loud voice*, and *heartily* to *rejoyce*. The *Scriptures* make mention of *all this*, and *much more*, as I have quoted elsewhere sufficiently in *this Book*.

'Tis sad to hear what *whining*, *toting*, *yelling*, or *screeking* there is in many *Country Congregations*, as if the people were *affrighted*, or *distracted*. And all is for want of *such a way and remedy* as *This* is.

. . . .

The matter of 30, 40, 50, *or* 60 *pounds* will procure a *very good Instrument*, *fit* for most *little Churches*, and so accordingly in proportion for *greater*.

Therefore now chear up, the way is plain and easie, if you be *willing*, and dare but venture *thus much* upon the *account* of *Gods Service*, (supposing he has commanded you to this small, or great Tax.) Thus much for an Organ.

But now as to an *Organist*; *That* is such a *difficult business*, as I believe you'l think *absolutely impossible* ever to be obtained; a *constant Charge*! a *Terrible business*!

For how many *hundred Parish Churches* are there in *England*? and there must be so many *Organists* at a *yearly charge*, whereas when our Organ is once set up, a small matter will *maintain* it for ever; But as to the charge of an Organist, this is sad.

Now for your comfort know, that this is *ten times more easie* and *feasible* than that other of the *Organ*; and that after ye are once gotten into the way, you will have *Organists grow up amongst* you as your *Corn grows* in your *Fields*, without *much* of your *Cost*, and *less* of your *Care*.

Chap. VI.

How to procure an Organist.

The *certain way* I will propose shall be *This*: *viz*. First, I will suppose you have a *Parish Clark*, and such an one as is able to set and lead a *Psalm*, although it be never so *indifferently*.

Now *This* being granted, I may say, that *I will*, or any *Musick Master* will, or many more *Inferiours*, (as *Virginal-Players*, or many *Organ-makers*, or the like) I say, *any* of *those will teach such a Parish Clark* how to *pulse* or *strike most of our common Psalm-Tunes*, usually Sung in our *Churches*, for a *trifle*, (viz. 20, 30, or 40 *shillings;*) and *so well*, that he need *never* bestow more cost to perform *that Duty sufficiently* during his *life*.

This I believe no *judicious person* in the *Art* will *doubt of*. And *then*, when *this Clark* is *thus well accomplish'd*, he will be so *doated* upon by all the *pretty ingenuous Children*, and *Young men* in the *Parish*, that scarcely any of them, but will be begging now and then a *shilling* or *two* of their *Parents* to give the *Clark*, that he may *teach them* to *pulse a Psalm-Tune*; the which *any such Child* or *Youth* will be able to do in a *week* or *fortnights time very well*.

And then again each Youth will be as *ambitious* to *pulse that Psalm-Tune* in *publick* to the *Congregation*, and no doubt but shall do it *sufficiently well*.

And thus by *little* and *little*, the *Parish* in a short time will *swarm*, or abound with *Organists*, and sufficient enough for *that Service*.

For you must know, (and I intreat you to believe me) that (seriously) it is one of the most *easie pieces of performance* in all *Instrumental Musick*, to *pulse* one of our *Psalm-Tunes truly and well*, after a very little shewing upon an *Organ*.

The Clark likewise will quickly get in *his Money*, by *this means*.

And I suppose no Parent will *grutch it him*, but rather *rejoyce* in it.

. . . .

Chap. VIII.

Wheresoever you send your *Children to School*, (I mean to the *Grammar-School*) *indent* so with the *Master* that your *Children* shall be *taught one hour* every day to *Sing*, or one *half day* in every *week at least*, either by *himself*, or by some *Musick-Master* whom he should procure: And no doubt but (if you will pay for it) *the business* may be effected.

For there are divers who are able to *teach to Sing*, and many more would quickly be, if such a general course were determin'd upon *throughout the Nation*.

There would scarcely be a *Schoolmaster*, but would, or might be easily able *himself* to do the *business*, once in a quarter or half a year; and in a short time every *Senior Boy* in the School will be able to do it *sufficiently well*.

And this is the most *certain, easie, and substantial way*, that can possibly be advis'd unto.

And thus, as before I told you, how that your *Organists* would *grow* up amongst you, as your *Corn grew in the Fields*, so now (if such a course as *This* would be taken) will your *Quiresters increase* even into *swarms* like your *Bees in your Gardens*, by which means the next *Generation* will be plentifully *able* to follow St. *Paul's Counsel*, namely, *to teach and admonish one another in Psalms and Hymns, and spiritual Songs*, and to *Sing with a Grace in their hearts and voices unto the Lord*, and to the *setting forth of his glorious praise*.

. . . .

Now all *These Things* considered, and *Thus* concurring, how should it be doubted, but that we must necessarily have *Excellent*, and most *Exquisite Church-Musick?*

The truth is, I do not doubt it, but can say, *I Know*, and am *Assured* that we have, *in some Places*.

But this also I must needs say, that in *many*, or *most Places, it is Deficient, Low, Thin* and *Poor*; and the *Great Grief* is, in that it cannot possibly be *Better'd* or *Amended*. (*Rebus sic stantibus*) as the Constitution of things stand at present, except there be some *other way* found out for *its Assistance*, then now is.

Now here it may be demanded, what *way* that should, or might be?

The which to answer Rightly, can be done no better way then first to consider well, what may be the *Defect*; which still can be no better way done, or discerned, then by making a *Comparison*, betwixt the *Original Sampler*, and the *Sample*, and by observing how *They agree*, or *differ*, or what *likeness* or *unlikeness* there may be between *Them*.

The *Sampler* or *Pattern* is express'd before, *viz*. the *Cathedral Musick of King Solomon's Temple*.[2]

And here I confess I could make a *Long-comparative-Recital*, between what was *Then*, and what is *Now*; but I shall forbear *That* (in *This Place*) and leave it to the Considerations and Apprehensions of the *Learned and Skilfull* in the *Art*, and shall only

---

[2]Mace stated earlier in his discussion that King Solomon's choir "undoubtedly was *The Pattern* or *Original* from whence *All Cathedral Musick* was first *deriv'd*: and in *Allusion* to which it is still (even) *kept Alive*, or *used* to this day in *All Cathedrals: Yet Infinitely short* of what was *Then." Ibid.*, p. 21.

speak something to the *Defect.*

And as to *That,* it is most apparently to be seen, and in these two Respects.

First, By the *General Thinness* of most *Quires.* viz. the *Paucity* or *Small number* of *Clarks* belonging to *each Quire.*

Secondly, By the *Disability* or *Insufficiency* of *most of Those Clarks.*

Now the *Thinness* of our *Quires* will appear by This, *viz.* that in most *Quires* there is but allotted *One Man to a Part*; and by reason of *which* it is impossible to have *That Service* constantly performed, although but in a very ordinary manner, (*Thinly.* yea *very Thinly*) because that often by reason of *Sickness. Indispositions. Hoarceness. Colds. Business.* and many other *Accidents* and *necessary Occasions. Men must be Absent. Disabled.* or *Impedited* from doing *Their Duties*; so that at *such Times,* the *Service* must *suffer.* And such like *Accidents* happen too often.

Then again, 2dly. As to the *Insufficiency* of many of *Those* (*Few*) *elected Clerks*; it is likewise apparent, that very *Few of Them* are (or can possibly be) *Masters* in the *Art of Song.* or *Singing*; much less in the *Art of Musick* in general.

And except they be *Masters* in the Art of Singing, (which is no such *easie Task* as is vulgarly thought to be) *They* are *not* to be accounted *Fit* for the Performance of *That Choice Duty.* which is the *most Eminent Piece of Our Church Service.*

If therefore *These two Defects* were *Well Weighed.* and considered upon, *So,* as they might possibly be *Remedied*; doubtless our *Church-Musick* would be *Exceedingly much Refin'd.* and *Improved*; otherwise *Not.*

And now because it must needs seem a *Hard matter to Rectifie These two* so very *Great Difficulties.* in regard they proceed from an *Occult. Remote,* or seeming *undiscernable Cause*; I will first lay open *That unperceivable Cause.* and then shew how both *Those former Difficulties* may (very probably) be *Overcome.* or *Rectified.*

And as to this *Cause* of the *Thinness* and *mean performance* of our *Cathedral Musick* in the general;

I conceive it proceeds from nothing so much as from the *low Esteem,* and *great Disregard.* which *most People* have, and all along have had of *it. in These latter Ages.* since the first Institution *Thereof.*

The which may be well perceived, in that there is *Nothing.* or *very Little* (to be seen or heard of) *Given* from any *late Benefactors.* towards the *Augmenting* or *Maintaining* of *it.* since the first very *liberal* and *well-meaning Founders large Bounties* and *Donations*; which although *They* were *very large. liberal.* and *sufficient Then.* yet *They* are *Now* in a manner as it were *shrunk to Nothing*.

This *very Thing*, I say, must needs argue a general *Low*, *Slight*, and *Disregardless value or Esteem* had unto *This Service*.

Whereas (on the contrary) if we cast our Eyes about, into any *County*, *City*, *Town-Corporate*, or *University*, &c. we may soon find out *Numbers of late Benefactors* or *Donors*, to sundry and various intended *Good Ends and Purposes*.

As, *viz.* so much given for *Ever* (in *Good Lands*) towards the maintaining of a *Lecture*, a *Free-School*, an *Almes-house*, a *Fellowship*, a *Scholarship*, *Building of Churches*, *Chappels*, *Monuments*, or such like.

But still we see *This very Excellent*, and *most Glorious piece* of the *Church-Service*, to stand *Forlornly Thin*, and very *meanly accommodated* or *Provided* for.

No *Great-Rich-Men* (Living or Dying) in *These our latter Ages*, so much as *Thinking*, or taking the *Least Notice* of *its Absolute* and very *Great Necessities*, so as to *bequeath* some *small matter* towards *its Needfull Augmentation* and *Illustration*.

And that there is such an absolute *Necessity*, must needs appear if it shall be consider'd, what manner of *pittifull-low* and *mean Allowances* the *Poor Servants* of the *Church* (in such *Places*) are *Generally* forc'd to *Live* upon; where *Their Yearly Wages* are in some *Quires* not exceeding *eight*, *ten*, or *twelve pounds a year*; but none amounting to *One quarter* so much as may *sufficiently*, or *comfortably maintain such Officers*, according to the *Nature* or *Dignity* of *Their Places*, in *These our Excessively-heightened and Dear Times*.

Yet I do verily believe, that such *Stipends* or *Wages* might *plentifully suffice Them*, in *Those former Cheap Times*, when (as I have heard) *Good Wheat* was bought for 4 d. the *Bushel*; and so in proportion (doubtless) all other *Commodities* answerably *low-priz'd* and *Cheap*: And *Money Then* (on the contrary) at a *High value*.

So that (without all Question) such a *Provision* of *eight*, *ten*, or *twelve pounds a year*, was *Then* a very *Considerable*, *Ample* and *sufficient Provision*; whereas *Now*, All things being so mightily alter'd from *Cheapness* to *Dearness*, it must needs be judg'd a very *Low*, *Inconsiderable*, *Insufficient*, *Unbecoming* and *Uncomfortable Livelihood*, for such an *Officer of the Church*, who (according to the Exhortation of the Prophet *King David*) should *Sing chearfully unto God*, and *Heartily Rejoyce*.

But *Alas! Alas!* He or They have little *Heart* or *Courage*, in *These our Griping Dayes*, So to Do; but rather on the contrary, to make *Sow'r Faces*, and *Cry*, or *Roar out aloud*, and say, *Who will do us any Good?* &c. For *We* and our *Families* are almost *starv'd*.

And how should they be thought otherwise then well-nigh

starv'd; were it not for that *Notable piece* of *Connivance*, or *Contrivance* of the *worthy Prelates* and *Masters of our Churches*, who suffer *Them* to *Work* and *Labour* (otherwise) for Their necessary *Livelihoods*; some in *one Calling*, and some in *another*, viz. in the *Barbers Trade*, the *Shoe-makers Trade*, the *Taylors Trade*, the *Smiths Trade*, and divers other (some) more *Inferiour Trades* or *Professions*, (God knows.)

   These Things, although they seem to the *Eyes* of *some* very *commendable* and *plausible*; yet to *others Not*; who say, 'tis rather a kind of *Dishonour* to the *Function of a Church-man*, and his *Office*, &c.

   Yet I confess, considering the *urgent Necessity*; as First, That no more then *Statutable-denominated-Wages* can be had;

   Then 2dly. That *Meat*, *Drink*, *Cloaths*, and *House-Rent* must be had for *Themselves*, *Wives* and *Children*:

   Therefore of *Two Evils* the *Less* is always to be *chosen*.

   So that in *This Hard Case*, there is a seeming kind of *Necessity* (pleaded for) to make *Choice* of *such Men* into *Those Places*, as will *sing* so *well as They Can*, for *so much Money*, although they be of other *Trades* and *Professions*.

   And indeed *This* is the *Real*, *True*, and *Miserable Condition* of the *Church-Service*, (in *That kind*) and of *Those Poor-drudging-Clarks* of *Quires* generally at *This Day*, for *want* of some *Open-hearted-Good-willing-Benefactors*, to *This Choice Piece of the Service*.

THE EIGHTEENTH CENTURY

Thomas Walter

(1696-1725)

The musical scene in early-eighteenth-century America was one of considerable dissension concerning the practice of religious song. The Puritan way of singing metrical psalms in unison was supported by a group of traditionalists, and a method of "Regular singing," which we simply call singing by note, was proposed by a group of enlightened ministers, many of whom were, incidentally, compilers of books to teach such note-singing. It was not destined for the old practice of lining-out psalm tunes for congregations without tunebooks to survive in the face of the popular singing schools, especially since the traditional group could put forth only scriptural defenses for their practices, while the modernists added some amount of logic and satirical comparison.

To judge from the argument printed here, Walter and his fellow agitators — among whom can be numbered Thomas Symmes and John Tufts — were men of comparatively clear vision. Their attempts to quote Scripture against the traditionalists, however, show that they were as capable of empty similes, windy parallels, and misinterpretations of the Old Testament as were the opposition. Walter's sermon, *The Sweet Psalmodist of Israel*, published the year after the material quoted here, is filled with the same kind of bombast and misinformation as we see in the others printed during that period, regardless of which side of the musical argument their authors espoused.

SOME BRIEF
And very plain Instructions
For Singing *by* NOTE.[1]

MUSICK is the Art of Modulating Sounds, either with the Voice, or with an Instrument. And as there are Rules for the right Management of an Instrument, so there are no less for the well ordering of the Voice. And tho' Nature it self suggests unto us a Notion of Harmony, and many Men, without ary other Tutor, may

[1]Thomas Walter, *The Grounds and Rules of Musick Explained : Or an Introduction to the Art of Singing by Note. Fitted to the meanest Capacities.* (Boston: printed by J. Franklin for S. Gerrish, 1721), pp. 1-5.

be able to strike upon a few Notes tolerably [t]uneful; yet this bears no more proportion to a Tune composed and sung by the Rules of Art than the vulgar Hedge-Notes of every Rustic does to the Harp of *David.* Witness the modern Performances both in the Theatres and the Temple.

SINGING is reducible to the *Rules of Art:* and he who has made himself Master of a few of these Rules, is able at first *Sight* to sing Hundreds of New Tunes, which he never saw o[r] heard before, and this by the bare Inspection of the Notes, without hearing them from the Mouth of a Singer. Just as a Person who has learned all the Rules of *Reading.* is able to read any new Book, without any further Help or Instruction. This is a Truth, altho' known to, and proved by many of us, yet very hardly to be received and credited in the Country.

WHAT a Recommendation is this then to the following Essay, that our Instructions will give you that knowledge in Vocal Musick, whereby you will be able to sing all the Tunes in the World, without hearing of them sung by another, and being constrained to get them by heart from any other Voice than your own? We don't call him a *Reader.* who can recite *Memoriter* a few Pieces of the Bible, and other Authors, but put him to read in those Places where he is a Stranger, cannot tell *ten Words in a Page.* So is he not worthy of the Name of a Singer, who has gotten eight or ten Tunes in his Head, and can sing them like a *Parrot* by Rote and knows nothing more about them, than he has heard from the Voices of others; and shew him a Tune that is new and unknown to him, can't strike two Notes of it.

THESE Rules then will be serviceable upon a Threefold Account. First, they will instruct us in the right and true singing of the Tunes that are already in use in our Churches; which, when they first came out of the Hands of the Composers of them, were sung according to the Rules of the *Scale of Musick.* but are now miserably tortured, and twisted, and quavered, in some Churches, into an horrid Medly of confused and disordered Noises. This must necessarily create a most disagreeable Jar in the Ears of all that can judge better of Singing than these men, who please themselves with their own illsounding Echoes. For to compare small things with great, our *Psalmody* has suffered the like Inconveniences which our *Faith* has laboured under, in case it had been committed and trusted to the uncertain and doubtful Conveyance of *Oral Tradition.* Our Tunes are, for want of a Standard to appeal to in all our Singing, left to the Mercy of every unskillful Throat to chop and alter, twist and change, according to their infinitely divers and no less odd Humours and Fancies. That this is not true, I appeal to the Experience of those who have happened to be present in many of our Congregations, who will grant me, that there are no two Churches that sing alike. Yea, I have my self heard (for Instance) *Oxford* Tune sung in three Churches (which I purposely forbear to mention) with as much difference as there can possibly be between *York* and *Oxford*, or any two other different Tunes. Therefore any man that pleads with me for what they call the *Old Way*, I can confute him only by making this Demand, *What is the* OLD WAY? Which I am sure they cannot tell. For, one Town says, theirs is the true *Old Way*, another Town thinks the same of theirs, and so does a third of their Way of Tuning it. But let such men know from the Writer of this Pamphlet (who can sing all the various Twistings of the old Way, and that too according to the Genres of most of the Congregations as well as they can any one Way; which must therefore make him a better Judge than they are or can be;) affirms, that the Notes sung according to the *Scale and Rules of Musick*, are the true *old Way*. For some body or other did compose our Tunes, and did they (think ye) compose them by Rule or by Rote? If the latter, how came they pricked them down in our Psalm Books? And this I am sure of, we sing them as they are there pricked down, and I am as sure the Country People do not, Judge ye then, who is in the right. Nay, I am sure, if you would once be at the pains to learn our Way of Singing, you could not but be convinced of what I now affirm. But our Tunes have passed thro' strange *Metamorphoses* (beyond those of Ovid) since their first Introduction into the World. But to return to the Standard from which we have so long departed cannot fail to set all to rights, and to reduce the sacred Songs to their primitive Form and Composition.

AGAIN, It will serve for the Introduction of more Tunes into the Divine Service; and these, Tunes of no small Pleasancy and Variety, which will in a great Measure render this Part of Worship still more delightful to us. For at present we are confined to *eight or ten Tunes*, and in some Congregations to little more than half that Number, which being so often sung over, are too apt, if not to create a Distaste, yet at least mightily to lessen the Relish of them.

THERE is one more Advantage which will accrue from the Instructions of this little Book; and that is this, that by the just and equal *Timeing* of the Notes, our Singing will be reduced to an exact length, so as not to fatigue the Singer with a tedious Protrastion of the Notes beyond the compass of a Man's Breath, and the Power of his Spirit: A Fault very frequent in the Country, where I my self have twice in one Note paused to take Breath. This *keeping of Time* in Singing will have this Natural effect also upon us, that the whole Assembly shall begin and end every single Note, and every Line exactly together, to an Instant, which is a wonderful Beauty in Singing, when a great Number of Voices are together sounding forth the Divine Praises. But for the want of this, I have observed in many Places, one Man is upon this Note, while another is a Note before him, which produces something so hideous and disorderly, as is beyond Expression bad. And then the even, unaffected, and smooth sounding the Notes, and the Omission of those unnatural Quaverings and Turnings, will serve to prevent all that Discord and lengthy Tediousness which is so much a fault in our singing of Psalms. For much time is taken up in shaking out these Turns and Quivers; and besides, no two Men in the Congregation quaver alike, or together; which sounds in the Ears of a good Judge, like *Five Hundred* different Tunes roared out at the same time, whose perpetual interferings with one another, perplexed Jars, and unmeasured Periods, would make a Man wonder at the false Pleasure which they conceive is that which good Judges of Musick and Sounds cannot bear to hear.

Roger North

(ca.1651-1734)

Although a successful lawyer who was appointed Attorney-General to James II, Roger North found London life an increasingly uncomfortable mode of existence after that monarch's death. By the end of the century North had removed to a country estate, where he was to spend the last three decades of his life, active in matters of law, in writing, and in his beloved pursuit of music. Much of what he wrote, he recast after some years. The section quoted here is such a reconsidered assessment, coming from his second *Musicall Grammarian* on which he placed the date 1728. English religious music had taken many turns during North's life, from the French-influenced Chapel Royal style under Charles II to the austere negation of the period under William and Mary. Roger North's ideal remained close to the cathedral practice with which he had been familiar in London, even after the years of country residence.

Ecclesiasticall Musick[1]

The Ecclesiasticall Style, as all agree, makes the best musick. It is therefore fitt to inquire what reasons there are for it. One seems to be, that it is confined to a solemnity of ayre, and all levitys are excluded; therefore the harmony is incomparably set off, which in light ayres is in great measure lost; and the melody hath no less advantage, because the movements are distinct as well as ayery. And within this compass there is scope enough for variety, for there will be a power of swifter and slower both in dupla and tripla measures, without running wild as the usages of other kinds of musick are apt to doe. And wherin those are most wanton, that is in the tripla measure, the church ayres surpass all; for no sort of musick expresseth the majesty of a *grand pas* like the slow tripla, which, to diversifie upon fitt occasion, may inliven; but yet all are to keep within the bounds of decency, suiting the place and

---

[1]*Roger North on Music: Being a Selection from his Essays written during the years. c.1695-1728.* Transcribed from the Manuscripts and edited by John Wilson (London: Novello and Co., 1959), pp. 266-71. Reproduced by permission of the publishers, Novello & Co. Ltd., London.

intention. This is the standard of our Church Musick; and if, as they say, consorts and operas are introduced in some forrein churches, it is in the place of anthems, and belong to the theatricall kind (of which afterwards), being intended for publik entertainement; and are no part of the service, as the hymnes and psallmodys are, which must retein their solemnity. And if the anthemes were as ours are, they might retein their appellation ecclesiasticall, which would not suffer by the greatest apparatus of voices and instruments that can be had, the style onely [being] altered, and that, as many will judge, for the better.

Another reason why Church Musick is preferred is because it is comonly heard in full chorus, or else in consort harmony, as in the dayly hymnes according to the best services, when the chorus sometimes pauseth, and then a consort of 3 or 4 voices continues the musick, till the chorus joynes againe. Here is a body of melody and harmony to fullfill the sharpest appetite to musick. Some may choose a superlative voice, to an exquisite *basso continuo*. and think that best. I grant it is wonderfully delightfull, but then 2 such voices are better, and 3 than those. I have not knowne any musick so exquisite as 2 prime voices in consort, and from thence I had an idea of more added, the bright clangor of which must needs kill any single voice; but being disposed consort-wise, . . . mixt with some pauses, and so junto and solo alternatively, is a consort in perfection, unless a consort of many such, if it were to be heard, should claim that caracter.

Another advantage which Church Musick hath, is the place; that is a spacious church, repleat with eccho, the very extent of which gives liberty to the sounds, as well as to soften, as to intermix. And I cannot allow that the musick proper for a great church would be so good in a chamber, for there the harmony would appear more broken, and all the roughnesses, and defects of the voices be more perceivable than in the church. And for the softening and polishing [of] the composition of the musicall sounds that arrive at the sence all together, there is a very apposite experiment which may be made at any time in King's Colledge Chappell. Between the shell of the main arches and the timber covering, lay an ear to one of the holes thro' which cords pass for carrying chaires when the inside of the roof is cleaned, and the organ with the Quire sounding, such a delicious musick shall be heard, as I may call the quintessence of Harmony, not otherwise to be described.

There is another means that advanceth the effect of Church Musick, and that is the magnificace of the structure in which it is heard. I challenge any one to say that he enters into a stately cathedrall and a barn, be it never so bigg, with the same temper of mind; for the former will strike a reverence, and raise the mind with a pleasure unknowne elsewhere. And if the walls have such effect upon the spiritts, the sounds within them, whether reading or singing, will partake in the same influence. The very organ is not the same thing as in a chamber, and the voices also excell; for where every thing resents[a] grandure, it would be strange if musick should not have its share. Besides all this, much is ascribed to the loudness of quire musick, for it is seldome that so many voices are heard together; even theaters and operas doe not afford it, of which afterwards. And now setting aside all these advantages, I must place the very manner and style of Church Musick, tho' [it were] confined to an ordinary chamber, in the front of all that's excellent in the whole survey of Harmony.

But I shall be asked what is the reason that these excellences are not found in many (if in any) of our cathedrall churches, so that except in Paul's, and the Royall Chappell, there are few that care much to hear it. I wish there were not reasons plenty to be given for it; I shall touch but a few particulars, and first as to the chanting of the Psalmes. When performed decently, the organ presiding, the musick, tho' it chant most upon the key note, yet in vertue of the cadences which are artificiall, the harmony is exceeding good. But one may conceive how it might be much better, if the English language would allow it; and that is if the whole quire should pronounce the verse as well as the close in distinct counterpoint time, with respect to long and short syllables, and then come off in the cadences all exactly together. But [even] where the most deliberate chanting is, the pronounciation is at best a huddle unintelligible, as if all strove to have done first. And for this reason, where the organ is not used which keeps the quire upright, the chanting is scandalous, such a confused din as no one living not pre-instructed could guess what they were doing; and I suppose the monks where Erasmus came, chanted in that manner, which provoked him to say, their sound was more like the gaggling of geese, than the voices of men. And with us, considering how litle (or rather no) care is taken of this noble part of the service, but all run on *non passibus equis*, it is a wonder that where the organ is used, it is so well performed as it is; and where it is not used, who expects better than the musick of Babell?

---

[a] = 'experiences' or 'feels'.

The Liturgie allows some passages to be *sayd or sung.* [and] one would consider the difference. It seems not to be so much as is commonly understood; for in that sence *singing* is not according to melody and harmony, but in a distinct and sonorous voice without any modulation at all, as the use is in our great churches in rehearsing the *Pater Noster* and *Credo:* and in that respect onely, *singing* differs from common speech. For in speech the syllables are pronounced close, and in a customable disorder; but in singing, every syllable is pronounced at length, and in the same musicall tone; and [it] doth not necessarily implye an harmonious composition. And if one may be so bold to guess, the singing the Niceen Creed as if it were an hymne proceeds from hence, for the requiring it to be *sung* doth not imply melodiously, but distinctly and with a sonorous voice all in the same tone; but our usage in the Second Service [Communion Service] is otherwise. And the true reason of vocall pronounciation in Great Churches, is that such vast congregations as were, or should be there, might hear and be edifyed, which would not be by comon speaking; and one may defie a good reader there to make himself well heard, unless he useth that manner which is called singing, and he shall fall into it incogitanter. Hence wee have also a rationale of changing the tone, for by that the remoter people might know what the prayers are, and also, by the cadence tone at the end, when the prayer is done; so also for the suffrages. The churches (generally) performe these parts well and in good order, and I have sayd thus much concerning them, purely in opposition to the stupid Sectarys, who suppose singing to be a light exercise, and unfitt for churches.

But it is very much to be lamented, that musicall skill and abillity is so low, that it is very hard to get voices to make a Quire. If most children were taught early, the best might be chosen; but if any grown up and untaught shew a good voice, then such are taken in, and with what difficulty taught? And how monstrous is the comon way of teaching comonly found to be, as hath bin already complained of? Wee will not complain of the great master, the Organist, who must needs be Doctor's standing; nor of the failings of the men Quiristers, among whom is rarely found a tollerable voice; nor mention the taking from the cathedralls the most hopefull of their boys, to serve in the Royal Chappells. But it is certein the Quires are poorly furnished, and one way or other the vocall performances are mean. And I think an observation of Good King Charles II at Canterbury, may conclude this topick. He was asked how he liked Dr Gosling's voice, and he answered that all the rest sang like Geese to him. One might without a desperate solescisme maintain that if female quiristers were taken into quires instead of boys, it would be a vast improvement of chorall musick, because they come to a judgment as well as voice, which the boys doe not arrive at before their voices perish, and small improvement of skill grows up in the room, till they come to man's estate. But both text and morallity are against it; and the Romish usage of castration is utterly unlawfull, and a scandallous practise wherever it is used.

Johann Sebastian Bach

(1685-1750)

In an age that often sees performances of the large Bach works by the choral societies of colleges and universities, or of a few fortunate lavishly endowed churches, supported by orchestral groups of various sizes, in which soprano and alto solos are sung by fully developed female voices with a wide range of experience at the command of the performers, and in which the instrumentalists are either competent professionals or amateurs who have rehearsed over a long period of time, we are likely to forget the difficulties that beset the composer of those works in his final — and in some respects, best — place of employment. Bach's constant differences with the officials of the Thomaskirche are well known. The complete set of documents that illuminates the life and times of that man who was destined to continue a dying tradition in the face of public demand for the modern style is available in *The Bach Reader*, the excellent collection from which the following memorandum is taken. That it should have been necessary for Bach to explain to the Town Council of Leipzig the problems of music-making in the churches of that city surely serves as evidence of gross neglect or lack of interest on their part. The need for improvement is evident at every point in Bach's document, but apparently no steps were taken to change the situation.

"SHORT BUT MOST NECESSARY DRAFT FOR A WELL-APPOINTED CHURCH MUSIC; WITH CERTAIN MODEST REFLECTIONS ON THE DECLINE OF THE SAME"[1]

A well-appointed church music requires vocalists and instrumentalists.

The vocalists are in this place made up of the pupils of the Thomas-Schule, being of four kinds, namely, sopranos (*Discantisten*), altos, tenors, and basses.

---

[1] Source: Reprinted from *The Bach Reader*. Edited by Hans T. David and Arthur Mendel. By permission of W. W. Norton & Company, Inc. Copyright 1966, 1945 by W. W. Norton & Company, Inc., pp. 120-24.

In order that the choruses of church pieces may be performed as is fitting, the vocalists must in turn be divided into 2 sorts, namely, concertists and ripienists.

The concertists are ordinarily 4 in number; sometimes also 5, 6, 7, even 8; that is, if one wishes to perform music for two choirs (*per choros*).

The ripienists, too, must be at least 8, namely, two for each part.

The instrumentalists are also divided into various kinds, namely, violinists (*Violisten*), oboists, flutists, trumpeters, and drummers. N.B. The violinists include also [i.e., in addition to the players of the violin] those who play the violas, the violoncellos, and the bass viols (*Violons*).

The number of the *Alumni Thomanae Scholae* [resident students of the Thomas-Schule] is 55. These 55 are divided into 4 choirs, for the 4 Churches in which they must perform partly concerted music with instruments, partly motets, and partly chorales. In the 3 Churches, St. Thomas's, St. Nicholas's, and the New Church, the pupils must all be musical. The Peters-Kirche receives the remainder, namely those who do not understand music and can only just barely sing a chorale.

Every musical choir should contain at least 3 sopranos, 3 altos, 3 tenors, and as many basses, so that even if one happens to fall ill (as very often happens, particularly at this time of year, as the prescriptions written by the school physician for the apothecary must show) at least a double-chorus motet may be sung. (N.B. Though it would be still better if the classes were such that one could have 4 singers on each part and thus could perform every chorus with 16 persons.) This makes in all 36 persons who must understand *musicam*.

The *instrumental music* consists of the following parts, namely:

2 or even 3 for the	*Violino* 1
2 or 3 for the	*Violino* 2
2 for the	*Viola* 1
2 for the	*Viola* 2
2 for the	*Violoncello*
1 for the	*Violon*[e]
2, or, if the piece requires, 3, for the	*Hautbois*
1, or even 2, for the	*Basson*
3 for the	*Trumpets*

1 for the	*Kettledrums*

summa   18 persons at least, for the instrumental music

N.B. If it happens that the church piece is composed with flutes also (whether they are *à bec* [recorders] or *Traversieri* [transverse flutes]), as very often happens for variety's sake, at least 2 more persons are needed. Making altogether 20 instrumentalists. The number of persons engaged for the church music is 8, namely, 4 Town Pipers (*Stadt Pfeifer*), 3 professional fiddlers (*Kunst Geiger*), and one apprentice. Modesty forbids me to speak at all truthfully of their qualities and musical knowledge. Nevertheless it must be remembered that they are partly *emeriti* and partly not at all in such *exercitio* as they should be.

The list is as follows:

Mr. Reiche	1st *Trumpet*
Mr. Genssmar	2nd *Trumpet*
vacant	3rd *Trumpet*
vacant	*Kettledrums*
Mr. Rother	1st *Violin*
Mr. Beyer	2nd *Violin*
vacant	*Viola*
vacant	*Violoncello*
vacant	*Violon[e]*
Mr. Gleditsch	1st *Hautbois*
Mr. Kornagel	2nd *Hautbois*
vacant	3rd *Hautbois*
	or *Taille*
The Apprentice	*Basson*

Thus there are lacking the following most necessary players, partly to reinforce certain voices, and partly to supply indispensable ones, namely:

    2 *Violinists* for the 1st *Violin*
    2 *Violinists* for the 2nd *Violin*
    2 that play the *Viola*
    2 *Violoncellists*
    1 *Violonist*
    2 for the *Flutes*

The lack that shows itself here has had to be supplied hitherto partly by the *studiosi* [of the University] but mostly by the *alumni* [of the Thomas-Schule]. Now, the *studiosi* have shown themselves willing to do this in the hope that one or the other would in time receive some kind of reward and perhaps be favored with a *stipendium* or *honorarium* (as was indeed formerly the custom). But since this has not occurred, but on the contrary, the few slight *beneficia* formerly devoted to the *chorus musicus* have been successively withdrawn, the willingness of the *studiosi*, too, has disappeared; for who will do work or perform services for nothing? Be it furthermore remembered that, since the 2nd *Violin* usually, and the *Viola*, *Violoncello*, and *Violone* always (in the absence of more capable *subjecti*) have had to be played by students, it is easy to estimate how much the chorus has been deprived of in consequence. Thus far only the Sunday music has been touched upon. But if I should mention the music of the Holy Days (on which days I must supply both the principal Churches with music), the deficiency of indispensable players will show even more clearly, particularly since I must give up to the other choir all those pupils who play one instrument or another and must get along altogether without their help.

Moreover, it cannot remain unmentioned that the fact that so many poorly equipped boys, and boys not at all talented for music, have been accepted [into the school] to date has necessarily caused the music to decline and deteriorate. For it is easy to see that a boy who knows nothing of music, and who cannot indeed even form a second in his throat, can have no natural musical talent; and *consequenter* can never be used for the musical service. And that those who do bring a few precepts with them when they come to school are not ready to be used immediately, as is required. For there is no time to instruct such pupils first for years, until they are ready to be used, but on the contrary: as soon as they are accepted they are assigned to the various choirs, and they must at least be sure of *measure* and *pitch* in order to be of use in divine service. Now if each year some of those who have accomplished something *in musicis* leave the school and their places are taken by others who either are not yet ready to be used or have no ability whatsoever, it is easy to understand that the *chorus musicus* must decline. For it is notorious that my honored *praeantecessores*, Messrs. Schell and Kuhnau, already had to rely on the help of the *studiosi* when they wished to produce a complete and well-sounding music; which, indeed, they were enabled to this extent to do, that not only some vocalists, namely, a bass, a tenor, and even an alto, but also instrumentalists, especially two violinists, were favored with separate *stipendia* by A Most Noble and Most Wise Council, and thus encouraged to reinforce the musical performances in the churches. Now, however, that the state of music is quite different from what it was, since our artistry has increased very much, and the *gusto* has changed astonishingly, and accordingly the former style of music no longer seems to please our ears, and considerable help is therefore all the more needed, in order to choose and appoint such musicians as will satisfy the present musical taste, master the new kinds of music, and thus be in a position to do justice to the composer and his work—now the few *beneficia*, which should have been rather increased than diminished, have been withdrawn entirely from the *chorus musicus*. It is, anyhow, somewhat strange that German musicians are expected to be capable of performing at once and *ex tempore* all kinds of music, whether it come from Italy or France, England or Poland, just as may be done, say, by those virtuosos from whom the music is written and who have studied it long beforehand, indeed, know it almost by heart, and who, *quod notandum*, receive good salaries besides, so that their work and industry thus is richly rewarded; while, on the other hand, this is not taken into consideration, but they [German musicians] are left to look out for their own wants, so that many a one, for worry about his bread, cannot think of improving—let alone distinguishing—himself. To illustrate this statement with an example one need only go to Dresden and see how the musicians there are paid by His Royal Majesty; it cannot fail, since the musicians are relieved of all concern for their living, free from *chagrin*, and obliged each to master but a single instrument: it must be something choice and excellent to hear. The conclusion is accordingly easy to draw, that with the stopping of the *beneficia* the powers are taken from me to bring the music into a better state.

In conclusion I find it necessary to append the enumeration of the present alumni, to indicate the skill of each *in musicis*, and thus to leave it to riper reflection whether in such circumstances the music can continue to be maintained, or whether its still greater decline is to be feared. It is, however, necessary to divide the whole group into three classes. Accordingly those who are usable are as follows:

(1) Pezold, Lange, Stoll, *Praefecti*. Frick, Krause, Kittler, Pohlreüter, Stein, Burckhard, Siegler, Nitzer, Reichhard, Krebs *major* and *minor*. Schönemann, Heder, and Kietel.

The names of the motet singers, who must first have further training in order to be used eventually for figured music, are as follows:

(2) Jänigke, Ludewig *major* and *minor*. Meissner, Neücke . . . . . *major* and *minor*. Hillmeyer, Steidel, Hesse, Haupt, Suppius, Segnitz, Thieme, Keller, Röder, Ossan, Berger, Lösch, Hauptmann, and Sachse.

Those of the last group are not *musici* at all, and their names are:
  (3) Bauer, Gross, Eberhard, Braune, Seyman, Tietze, Heben-
      streit, Wintzer, Össer, Leppert, Haussius, Feller, Crell,
      Zeymer, Guffer, Eichel, and Zwicker.
Total: 17 usable, 20 not yet usable, and 17 unfit.

JOH. SEB. BACH
Leipzig, August 23, 1730   *Director Musices*

Pope Benedict XIV

(1675-1758)

The instructions relative to music that issued from Rome reflected, in each generation, a danger from the secular world. By the middle of the eighteenth century, this danger was the theatrical world, the attractions of which were centered in the opera house. References to solo and small ensemble singing, to instruments other than strings and bassoon, and to the fact that even those, along with the organ, were tolerated and not invited, imply a deep erosion of plainsong tradition. The document of 1665 was concerned with choral music in general; this one is concerned with accompaniment and theatrical effect. We shall see in the next such document (page 143)) that the emphasis shifts to musical style.

Encyclical Letter of Pope Benedict XIV[1] (February 19, 1749)

Résumé

1. The Canonical Hours must be sung by those whose duty it is to do so, with gravity and with devotion. The Gregorian Chant must be rendered in perfect unison and must be directed by persons who are competent. *This Chant arouses devotion, and, when well rendered, it gives greater joy to devout persons than figured music.*

2. Figured music is permitted in Church, and even with accompaniment by the organ or other instruments, provided that this music be neither profane, worldly nor theatrical in character, but be of such nature as to arouse among the faithful, sentiments of piety and devotion and to uplift the soul toward God.

3. The sacred text must be put to music in such a way that the words remain perfectly and clearly intelligible.

4. Ecclesiastical music must be composed in a style which differs from that of the theatre. The solo, the duet, the trio, etc.,

[1] *Papal Documents on Sacred Music*, p. 5. Reprinted by permission of *Sacred Music*, Journal of The Church Music Association of America.

are forbidden.

5. The custom is *tolerated* in those places where it has already been introduced, of playing the organ or other instruments in Church, apart from the mere accompaniment of the Chant, but on condition that this instrumental music be grave, serious and different in style from theatrical music. These instrumental pieces must not be long.

6. Apart from the organ, the instruments which are tolerated are: stringed instruments and *fagotti*. Those which are forbidden are: *timpani* (kettledrums), hunting horns, trumpets, oboes, flutes, *Salteri*, mandolins, and, in general, all instruments which are theatrical in character.

7. Instrumental accompaniment of the singing must not overpower the voices, but must serve to intensify the expression of the words and *increase the love of God.*

John Alcock

(1715-1806)

The cathedral system of England undertook the training of children and often brought them, as mature musicians, into the field of church music where they, in turn, trained others to follow in their footsteps. John Alcock was familiar with the problems of eighteenth-century English church music. He was a church musician from age seven, when he began as a chorister at St. Paul's Cathedral under Charles King, until his declining years, when he relinquished all duties save those of lay-vicar. He achieved recognition as an organist and composer. His greatest importance now lies in his sharp reflection of the ills of his own time. His compositions are typical of the uninspired church fare that was current during his life; his comments about the condition of choirs and their effectiveness may be accepted as those of a man who has hoped for the best and experienced the worst. There is no evidence that conditions at Lichfield Cathedral improved during Alcock's lifetime. However, Maria Hackett, in *A brief account of cathedral and collegiate schools* . . . (London: J. Nichols and son, 1827), indicates that the original number of choristers had been restored. Whether the dignity of the organist among the adult singers was elevated to its proper place is not clear. The dedication to his Service is printed in its entirety.

Dedication from A Morning and Evening Service, . . . [1]

To the Reverend Dr. *Addenbrooke*. Dean of the Cathedral of Lichfield

Sir,

The following *Service*, tho' the first of my compositions, will, I hope, be thought not altogether unworthy your Patronage. It has been my chief Endeavour, in the Setting of these *Sacred Hymns*, to preserve such a Gravity in the *Melody* as may best tend to excite a true Spirit of Devotion in the Hearers. And here I cannot omit

---

[1]Source: John Alcock, *A Morning and Evening Service, consisting of a Te Deum, Jubilate, Kyrie-eleison, Nicene Creed, Magnificat and Nunc dimittis:* . . . (London: Printed for the Author and Jno. Johnson, 1752), (pp. iii-iv).

just mentioning, how happy we of this *Choir* ought to think ourselves, who, besides the Allowance of a comfortable Maintenance, are blest with a *Bishop. Dean. &c.* whose whole Study and Delight are the Advancement of Religion, and the Good of this *Church:* and whose Example, if sufficiently attended to by us, wou'd soon make this *Cathedral* a glorious Temple of Divine Worship; whereas, on the contrary, I may venture to affirm, no *Choir* in the Kingdom is so much neglected by the Members thereof as this; one of them attending no more than five Weeks in a Year, another five Months, some seven, and few of them so often as they might do; sometimes only one Priest-Vicar at *Church.* and at other Times, but one Lay-Vicar, both on *Sundays* as well as the Week-Days, tho' there are Eleven of them, which has occasion'd some People of the Town to write upon the *Church* Doors, *My House shall be called the House of Prayer. but ye have made it a Den of Thieves.* As to myself, I am so far from thinking my Duty a Slavery, as, (God forgive them) too many seem to do, that I really esteem it, as it certainly is, not only a reasonable, but also a delightful Service; and my Regard for *Cathedral Music* is so great, that I profess I know nothing upon Earth exceeds it, when performed with *Decency* and *Judgment.* which is what I still live in Hopes of hearing, as I'm persuaded, by numberless Circumstances, no Motive will be wanting on your Part, to promote this heavenly Exercise, whenever Vacancies shall happen: And that you will then make Choice of those Persons who, beside having a competent Knowledge in Music, shall have good Voices, and such as are at that Time most wanted, whether *Contratenor. Tenor.* or *Bass.* If the Singers are not skill'd in the Musical Part of their Duty, Disputes must unavoidably arise betwixt them and the Organist; for the natural Consequence is, that when they sing wrong, the Fault is laid on him, no Matter how great his Merit is; and he having no one to appeal to that understands Music, the former of course get the better of the latter, as it generally happens in these Cases, that those People who make the greatest Noise, and talk most fluently, are thought to have the true Side of the Argument, especially if they are perfectly acquainted with the Nack of Lying *judiciously:* And this is done with an artful View of setting the *Dean* and *Chapter* against the Organist, in order that they may have a Pretence for absenting themselves from Church; and very often this Scheme, vile as it is, succeeds according to their Wishes. I can't forbear relating one very extraordinary Thing I have heard a certain Pretender to Music advance, tho' rather too ridiculous to trouble you with, which is, that the Organist, in the *Services* and

Anthems, shou'd always keep with the Singers, so that if one sings extremely slow, another extremely fast, and others moderately, all at one Time, (which is what I have frequently heard,) he must nevertheless play with each of them. In all the *Cathedrals* and Chapels Abroad, the Organist is always look'd upon as the *Maestri de Capella,* or Master of the Chapel; and so I think they shou'd be in *England,* if they are eminent in their Profession, and then we shou'd not have *Services* and *Anthems* for six Voices put up, when there are only three Singers in the *Choir* to perform them. I knew a Man (some time since) who pass'd for a famous Singer, and got surprising Preferment, that had learnt about seven *Anthems* when he was a Boy, in a pretty Taste, and sung them all his Life-time with universal Applause, tho' he cou'd not take off a common Ballad at first Sight to his dying Day, and yet would find fault with every Organist that accompanied him. I wou'd not by this be understood, that I think it absolutely necessary for every Singer to be a compleat Master of Music, or do I contemn any one for not understanding it, but surely it wou'd be but Prudence in such, not to set up for Critics in a Science they are utter Strangers to; however, it is a well known Maxim, that Pride and Ignorance constantly attend each other.

    I am, Sir,

       With the utmost Respect,

          Your most Dutiful Vicar, and Organist,

             John Alcock.

Lichfield Close,
Sept. 15, 1753.

James Lyon

(1735-1794)

American collections of psalm-tunes had become fairly common by the second half of the eighteenth century, but it was not until the publication of Lyon's *Urania* that one of them contained original compositions by an American. Lyon's significant musical activity is confined to this one volume, if we are to judge by extant examples, although there is some evidence that he was active in music most of his life. He composed an ode for the commencement exercises at the College of New Jersey (later Princeton University) in 1759, the year he received his Bachelor of Arts degree. *Urania* dates from two (or, less likely, three) [1] years later. The dedicatory material accurately forecasts the combination of pious and mercenary aims that succeeding collections were to pursue.

Dedication to Urania [2]

To
The Clergy of every Denomination
in America

Reverend Sirs,

RELYING on the evident Propriety of your patronizing this Publication, permit me to lay URANIA at your feet.

Should the following Collection of Tunes be so fortunate, as to merit your Approbation; To please the Taste of the Public; To assist the private Christian in his daily Devotion; And to improve, in any degree, an important Part of Divine Service in these Colonies, for which it was designed: I shall think myself happy in

---

[1] Bibliographers generally credit the year 1761 with its publication; however, Gilbert Chase, *America's Music: From the Pilgrims to the Present* (New York: McGraw-Hill Book Company, Inc., 1955), p. 126, gives the date as 1762. Lyon's place in American music, and the historical importance of *Urania*, are discussed in Elwyn A. Wienandt and Robert H. Young, *The Anthem in England and America* (New York: The Free Press, 1970).

[2] Source: James Lyon, *Urania, or a Choice Collection of Psalm-Tunes, Anthems, and Hymns . . .* (Philadelphia: H. Dawkins, 1761), pp. ii-iii.

being the Editor, notwithstanding the great Expence, Labour, and Anxiety, it has cost me to compleat it.

MAY YOU long continue Ornaments of your Profession: Daily see abundant Fruits of your Labour in the Reformation of Mankind: And incessantly enjoy those sublime Pleasures, which nothing, but a Series of rational and virtuous Actions, can create.

I am,

Reverend Gentlemen,

Your most obedient,

and humble Servant,

JAMES LYON.

William Hayes

(1741-1790)

Although he appears to be the least important of the Hayes family of musicians, contributing nothing in the way of original music, this third son of a more widely known father of the same name has left an interesting document which reflects the frustrations of church musicians in the latter half of the eighteenth century. He seems to have been more mobile than many of his profession, a situation that may have been brought about through such public utterances as the open letter printed here. He moved to Magdalen College in 1764, to Worcester Cathedral in 1765 (the year of this set of rules), and to St. Paul's in London the following year. It is interesting to speculate whether he moved from Worcester or to St. Paul's as a result of the publication, the signature of which is so thinly disguised as to invite discovery.

"Rules necessary to be observed by all Cathedral-Singers in this Kingdom."[1]

In the first place every singer should take particular care to observe a proper plainess in singing; for, as too much finery adds no ornament to a beautiful personage, but has a quite contrary effect, so too much gracing of a musical composition, often ends in a total *disgracing*. There seems to be the *cantandi simplicitas* in the latter, as well as the *simplicitas munditia* in the former.[a]

---

[1] William Hayes, "Rules Necessary to be observed . . .," *The Gentleman's Magazine, and Historical Chronicle,* XXXV (May, 1765), pp. 213-14.

[a] There are several parts of cathedral musick which can never be sung and accompanied with too much simplicity and plainess. To instance in one particular, i.e. the *Vouchsafe O Lord,* in *Purcell's Te Deum.* If singer and accompanier would do justice to this strain, I would advise them to use nothing but the *appogiatura,* and even that with great caution and reserve. But instead of this I have often had the misfortune of hearing the greatest part of it smother'd (for what else can I call it?) with such a farrago of superfluities, that between singer and player they have almost made a very tolerable country dance of it.

It very often happens that there is more difficulty in the application than in the formation of a grace. The inventive faculty of a singer may be awake when his judgement is quite fast asleep. This is often the case with many instrumental performers, who, instead of doing justice to a *Handel,* a *Corelli,* and a *Geminiani,* are often playing a great number of surprising tricks, to the no small injustice of the authors.

With regard to a long grace at the end of any part of an anthem, I think it should be very cautiously avoided, because it breaks in too much upon the seriousness and dignity of church musick. But if a singer should be determined to favour a congregation with a *gratioso*.[b] I would advise the organist to play a little short voluntary as soon as the grace is quite finished, in order to qualify the singer to go on with a *quantum sufficit* of breath for the remaining part of the anthem, because there are so many twistings and twinings, so many instantaneous ups and downs in a thing of this sort, that the *arteria aspera* is often put into a sort of convulsive motion, and more particularly so when this said grace requires a considerable degree of vocal velocity, *sed hoc obiter notandum est.*

The power of the organist in a full chorus seems to be of a despotick nature. He is the *primum mobile.* Every singer must constantly hearken to the organ. In the nature of things it cannot be otherwise.[c] You'll say, perhaps, that the organist may be deficient sometimes with regard to time: — it is granted; — and so may the greatest performer: a *Handel* may vary with respect to time, and be a *Handel* still! But suppose the organist is not always regular, yet it is the business of the whole choir to attend to him.[d] In other parts of cathedral musick, (such as a solo and duett) the organist may humour the singer, and the singer the organist, in case both of them are well conversant in compliance and good nature. But when I talk of compliance between player and singer it is certainly more practicable in a solo than any other part of church musick.

With regard to the leading of *a point* in a chorus,[e] every

---

b   i.e. Any part of an anthem, where the singer is not relieved by an additional symphony of the composer: In this case the organist may omit the voluntary, because the symphony will make up the deficiency, and answer the very same purpose. As for the conclusion, the singer is relieved of course by the chorus.

cAlthough the power of the organist, in a full chorus, savours very strongly of despotism, yet in other parts of church-musick it partakes of the nature of a mixed limited monarchy; *i.e.* in harmony he seems monarchical, but not in melody.

dIt ought to be considered that the organist has always the most difficult task to engage in. The singer has only his respective part to attend to, whereas the organist is obliged to observe the whole of the harmony, for which reason any little deviation in point of time may happen, even to the most skillful performer. But there is another very good reason to be assigned why the organist is particularly to be attended in a full chorus, because in case of any mistake, it is easy for a single part to come into the whole, but the whole cannot come into a part: Those who understand musick will easily perceive what I mean.

eMr *Beard* is the best singer of a chorus I ever heard. He attends to the organ, and is an excellent directory at any time to the whole of a musical performance. He is greatly to be admired (in like manner) in a recitative both of the common, and that of the accompanied one. He takes off that tœdium or weariness which such kind of composition is apt to cause upon the generality of an audience. But whether in some few instances he does not pay greater attention to the common speech (I am now speaking as to oratorios) than to tuneful pronunciation, is a thing which I shall not take upon me to determine. By the common recitative I mean mere speech, by the accompanied one, tuneful pronunciation.

member should exert his voice as much as the nature of his constitution will admit of. — The too frequent use of the swell is attended with bad consequences, unless the voice is extremely good; and where the voice is good (unless the singer is well conversant in the *ne plus ultra* of his windpipe) it very often degenerates into a sudden instantaneous bawl or squall.

The practice of singing the octave above instead of the octave below, (and so *vice versa*) has a very unnatural effect. Singers often take too much liberty in this respect, little considering that although it may be the same with regard to the laws of composition, yet there seems to be an obvious difference in nature.

Let me now give a short friendly hint or two to the organist.

If the organist would think it proper to play one of Mr *Handle's* fugues, sometimes (not but I propose this with all due submission) instead of a constant voluntary of his own, it is more than probable that such an innovation may bring no singular disgrace upon the character and reputation of an organist. Besides which it may border very near upon compassion and good nature to give an *innuendo* of this sort, in order to afford some friendly relief to the inventive faculty of the organist; because it may be very prejudicial and hurtful to the constitution to have the invention always upon the full stretch. But if the organist should persevere in extempore playing, (for the organ is an instrument finely calculated for it) it would be kind of the organist to keep to his fugue; and not only this, but to chuse one of a moderate length; because in this case the audience may probably remember the fugue, and consequently more easily digest the voluntary.[f] But there is one thing relative to the organist which I should have mentioned before, which is this, If the organist should transpose an anthem out of the original key of a composer (I mean at sight) in order to ease the voice of a singer, it would be prudent of the singer to thank him, the first opportunity, for such a compliance; because the organist, strictly speaking, is obliged to transpose out of the original key.

In the winter season the organist should never presume to play upon the organ in gloves, unless there is a great necessity for it.

But let me not be thought too presumptuous if I should give a little advice to the chantor.

If the chantor of every cathedral would read a short lecture

---

[f] It must be allowed that set compositions, how well soever executed upon an organ, will always have the appearance of stiffness (at least to a discerning and judicious ear) when compared with those which come voluntary from the mind. Extempore playing is certainly the thing, in case an organist will take some pains to excel.

upon the nature of harmonicks, or make a brief descant on several passages in church musick, such a method as this might be of great use to church musick, and at the same time add considerable weight and significancy to the office of chantor.

The chantor should have a correct score of all the musick that is performed in the church; and if a mistake should happen in a single part, such mistake should be constantly corrected from his score.

If the chantor desires a rehearsal of any musick, all the members must comply, and more particularly so if the chantor should desire it in a polite, genteel, and friendly manner.

But, after all, I believe it will be readily granted that the best manner of singing, either with graces or without them, will be of little or no consequence unless all the members are in peace and harmony one with another: With union of sound, therefore, it will be always necessary to join union of brotherly love and affection.

I am. Sir. &c.   W----M H-----s,
a Member of the Cathedral Church of
Worcester .

Leopold Mozart

(1719-1787)

Wolfgang Amadeus Mozart

(1756-1791)

The Mozarts left a wealth of correspondence. Their travels are partly the cause of the great number of letters, but not entirely, for many of them are simply exchanges of news, requests for shipment of scores or copying of parts, plans for music performances, reports of concerts heard, and so on.

Only a few of the letters discuss church music. Its style was rarely open to question; its practice was worth discussing only when it deviated from the norm. Other letters not printed here emphasize matters that were found by their writers to be interesting or amusing. It is not possible to build a continuous narrative by piecing together all the letters concerned with church music, but the entire set has the distinct advantage, on the other hand, of giving a picture of music for the Catholic Church as it was seen by trained Catholic musicians.

Part of a letter from Leopold Mozart to his son[1]

Salzburg, November 1st-3rd, 1777

Mon très cher Fils!

I have this moment come in from the Cathedral service, during which Haydn's oboe mass[a] was performed, he himself conducting it. He had also composed the offertory and, instead of a sonata, he had set to music the words of the graduale,[2] which the priest had

---

[1]Source: Emily Anderson, ed., *The Letters of Mozart & His Family* (3 vols.; London: Macmillan and Co., 1938), II, 515-16. The letters are printed in volume 1 of the two-volume edition, and are printed by permission of St. Martin's Press, Inc., and The Macmillan Co. of Canada Ltd., and Macmillan & Co., Ltd., London.

[a]Michael Haydn's mass which Leopold Mozart praises so highly is his so-called Hieronymus mass in C major, finished on September 14th, 1777.

[2]Later in this letter Leopold says that "the graduale was not by Haydn but by an Italian. Haydn had got it from [Johann Adam Karl Georg] Reutter some time or other."

to say. The mass was rehearsed yesterday after vespers. . . . I liked
the whole mass very much, as there were six oboists, three double
basses, two bassoons and the castrato *who has been taken on for six
months at one hundred gulden a month.*[b]. . . What I particularly liked
was that, since oboes and bassoons resemble very much the human
voice, the tutti seemed to be a very strongly supported chorus of
voices, as the sopranos and altos, strengthened by the six oboes and
the alto trombones, admirably balanced the number of tenor and
bass voices; and the pieno was so majestic that I could have easily
done without the oboe solos. The whole affair lasted an hour and a
quarter and I found it far too short, for it is really an excellent
composition. It all flows along naturally; the fugues, and
particularly the Et vitam etc. in the Credo, the Dona Nobis and
the Hallelujah in the offertory are worked out in a masterly
fashion, the themes being most natural and without any
exaggerated modulations or too sudden transitions. . . . I should
mention that Brunetti stood behind Ferlendis, Wenzl Sadlo[c]
behind the bassoon-players and Hafeneder behind the other
oboists. They watched Haydn throughout the performance and
beat time on their shoulders; otherwise it would have really gone
higgledy-piggledy in places and particularly in the fugues and in
the running bass-accompaniments. The result may be at last an
appointment as Cathedral Kapellmeister or Vice-Kapellmeister, for
which Haydn has been working for so many years.

Part of a letter from Wolfgang Mozart to his father[3]

Mannheim, November 4th, 1777

. . . .

Now I must tell you about the music here. On Saturday, All
Saints' Day, I was at High Mass in the Kapelle. The orchestra is
excellent and very strong. On either side there are ten or eleven
violins, four violas, two oboes, two flutes and two clarinets, two
horns, four violoncellos, four bassoons and four double basses, also
trumpets and drums. They can produce fine music, but I should

---

b Francesco Ceccarelli. [In an earlier footnote, Anderson writes in connection with his name in a letter
dated October 27, 1777, that "he was appointed soon afterwards to the Archbishop's service for six
years at an annual salary of 800 gulden."]
c Wenzl Sadlo played the horn in the Salzburg court orchestra. . . . [Gaetano Brunetti was a violinist
in the court orchestra, as was Joseph Hafeneder. Their employment as time-beaters is indicative of the
attention that was devoted to this performance.]
[3] Source: Anderson, *Letters of Mozart,* II, pp. 521-23.

not care to have one of my masses performed here. Why? On account of their shortness? No, everything must be short here too. Because a different style of composition is required? Not at all. But because, as things are at present, you must write principally for the instruments, as you cannot imagine anything worse than the voices here. Six sopranos, six altos, six tenors and six basses against twenty violins and twelve basses is just like zero to one. Is that not so, Herr Bullinger? The reason for this state of affairs is that the Italians are now in very bad odour here. They have only two castrati, who are already old and will just be allowed to die off. The soprano would actually prefer to sing alto, as he can no longer take the high notes. The few boys they have are miserable. The tenors and basses are like our funeral singers. Vice-Kapellmeister Vogler, who had composed the mass which was performed the other day, is a dreary musical jester, an exceedingly conceited and rather incompetent fellow.[a] The whole orchestra dislikes him. But to-day, Sunday, I heard a mass by Holzbauer, which he wrote twenty-six years ago, but which is very fine. He is a good composer, he has a good church style, he knows how to write for voices and instruments, and he composes good fugues. They have two organists here who alone would be worth a special visit to Mannheim.[b] I have had an opportunity of hearing them properly, for it is not the custom here to sing the Benedictus, but during that part of the service the organist has to play the whole time. On the first occasion I heard the second organist and on the second, the first organist. But in my opinion the second is even more distinguished than the first. For when I heard him, I enquired: "Who is playing the organ?" I was told, the second organist. He played abominably. When I heard the other one, I asked: "Who is playing now?" I was told, our first organist. He played even more wretchedly and I think that if they were thrown together, something even worse would be the result. To watch these gentlemen is enough to make one die of laughing. . . .

---

[a] Mozart had already sided with Vogler's opponents. For a good account of Mozart's relations with Vogler see Abert, [W. A. Mozart. Leipzig: 1923-34] vol. ii, pp. 982 ff.

[b] Nikolaus Bayer and Anton Marxfelder. The latter was organist in Manheim from 1745 until 1778.

Charles Burney

(1726-1814)

The two tours of Dr. Burney took him into the churches of many important Continental cities. His enthusiasm for musical performances and his pleasure in conversations on musical topics have provided a wealth of information about the contemporary scene both in the reports of his journeys and his history of music, the latter written as a direct outgrowth of the information gathered in the course of his two extended trips abroad. Burney was not simply a journalist who reported with a layman's outlook; he was a capable performer of keyboard instruments, and he had achieved some small success as a composer. His opinions are those of an informed man, probably as objective as it is possible to be in a large-scale evaluation.

Venice

August 6, 1770[1].

This morning the Doge went in procession to the church of S. *Giovanni e Paolo*. I was not only curious to see this procession, but to hear the music, which I expected would be very considerable, and by a great band; however there was only a mass sung in four parts, without other instrument than the organ, but then it was so good of the kind, so well executed and accompanied, that I do not remember ever to have received more pleasure from this kind of music. One of the organists of St. Mark's church, who is in orders, attended, and discovered himself, in his voluntaries and interludes, to be a very masterly performer.

The voices were well chosen, and well assorted, no one stronger than the other; the composition was of Lotti, and was truly grave and majestic, consisting of fugues and imitations in the stile of

[1]Source: Charles Burney, *The Present State of Music in France and Italy* (2nd ed., corrected; London: T. Becket and Co., 1773), pp. 151-53. An annotated reprint of this volume, and of Burney's subsequent two-volume report of his travels to Germany and adjacent countries, may be found in Percy A. Scholes (ed.), *Dr. Burney's Musical Tours in Europe* (2 vols.; London: Oxford University Press, 1959).

our best old church services, which have been so well selected, and
published in so magnificent a manner by Dr. Boyce: all was clear
and distinct, no confusion or unnecessary notes; it was even
capable of expression, particularly one of the movements, into
which the performers entered so well, that it affected me even to
tears.

The organist here very judiciously suffered the voices to be
heard in all their purity, insomuch that I frequently forgot that
they were accompanied; upon the whole this seems to be the true
stile for the church: it calls to memory nothing vulgar, light, or
prophane; it disposes the mind to philanthropy, and divests it of
its gross and sensual passions.

Indeed my being moved was the mere effect of well-modulated
and well-measured sounds, for I knew not the words, which were
wholly lost by the distance; nor is this species of music at all
favourable to poetry; in the answers that are made to the points,
the several parts all sing different words, so that no great effects
can be produced by them; but notwithstanding this defect, such
music as this, in the service of the church, must ever be allowed
to have its merit, however it may be exploded, or unfit for
theatrical purposes.

The Sistine Chapel

November 12, 1770[2]

I visited the Pope's, or Sistine chapel, and being a day in which
there was no service, I had permission to go into every part of it,
which I was curious to do on many accounts. First, as it is the
place in which the famous *Miserere* of Allegri is performed;
secondly, as it was here that church-music first had its rise, and
was brought to its highest perfections; and thirdly, where, at the
altar piece, is so wonderfully painted the last judgment: it is the
greatest work of Michael Angelo, and perhaps of man. Nothing
can be conceived more astonishing and dreadful than the ideas and
figures which his dark imagination has produced; neither the
Inferno of Dante, nor the hell of Milton, can furnish any thing
more terrible. But this amazing work is greatly discoloured, and
the ceiling, by the same painter, is in many places broken down
two or three feet in breadth. The sides are painted by Pietro

---

[2]Source: Burney, *The Present State of Music*, pp. 378-80.

Perugino, and are the best works that I have seen of this famous master of the divine Raphael.

I went into the orchestra with respectful curiosity, to see the place sacred to the works of Palestrina. It seems hardly large enough to contain thirty performers, the ordinary number of singers in the Pope's service; and yet, on great festivals, supernumeraries are added to these. There was nothing in the orchestra now but a large wooden desk for the score-book of the *Maestro di Capella*, and marble seats at the back and sides: it is placed on the right hand in approaching the altar, facing the Pope's throne, which is near the altar on the other side. There are seats or stalls for the cardinals at the sides of the chapel, and a small place for ambassadors to stand in, just within the rails opposite to the altar; but no other strangers are ever admitted; nor are any persons, except the performers, suffered to enter the orchestra during the service. The grate, or balustrade, which is in diamond squares, gilt, seems to take off one third of the whole room, which is very lofty and magnificent, but now very dusty and much out of repair; the floor is in beautiful Mosaic of marble.

Vienna

August 30-September 9, 1772 [3]

The first time I went to the cathedral of St. Stephen, I heard an excellent mass, in the true church style, very well performed; there were violins and violoncellos though it was not a festival. The great organ at the west end of this church has not been fit for use these forty years; there are three or four more organs of a smaller size in different parts of the church, which are used occasionally. That which I heard in the choir this morning is but a poor one, and as usual, was much out of tune; it was played, however, in a very masterly, though not a modern style. All the responses in this service, are chanted in four parts, which is much more pleasing, especially where there is so little melody, than the mere naked *canto fermo* used in most other catholic churches; the treble part was sung by boys, and very well; particularly, by two of them, whose voices, though not powerful, had been well cultivated.

. . . .
_____

[3]Charles Burney, *The Present State of Music in Germany, the Netherlands, and United Provinces* . . . (2 vols.; 2nd ed., corrected; London: T. Becket and Co., 1775), 1, 218-19; 225-27; 325-27; 333-34.

At night two of the poor scholars of this city sung, in the court of the inn where I lodged, duets in *falset. soprano.* and *contralto.* very well in tune, and with feeling and taste. I sent to enquire whether they were taught music at the Jesuits' college, and was answered in the affirmative. Though the number of poor scholars, at different colleges, amounts to a hundred and twenty, yet there are at present but seventeen that are taught music.

After this there was a band of these singers, who performed through the streets a kind of glees, in three and four parts: this whole country is certainly very musical. I frequently heard the soldiers upon guard, and centinels, as well as common people, sing in parts. The music school at the Jesuits' college, in every Roman catholic town, accounts in some measure for this faculty; yet other causes may be assigned, and, among these, it should be remembered, that there is scarce a church or convent in Vienna, which has not every morning its *mass in music:* that is, a great portion of the church service of the day, set in parts, and performed with voices, accompanied by at least three or four violins, a tenor and base, besides the organ; and as the churches here are daily crowded, this music, though not of the most exquisite kind, must, in some degree, form the ear of the inhabitants. Physical causes operate but little, I believe, as to music. Nature distributes her favours pretty equally to the inhabitants of Europe; but moral causes are frequently very powerful in their effects. And it seems as if *the national music of a country was good or bad. in proportion to that of its church service:* which may account for the taste of the common people in Italy, where indeed the language is more musical than in any other country of Europe, which certainly has an effect upon their vocal music; but the excellent performances that are every day heard for nothing in the churches, by the common people, more contribute to refine and fix the national taste for good music, than any other thing that I can at present suggest.

.   .   .   .

From hence, I went to St. Stephen's cathedral, where high mass was just begun; on account of its being the Nativity of the Virgin, the band was reinforced; there were more than the usual number of instruments, as well as voices; but the organ was insufferably out of tune, which contaminated the whole performance. In other respects, the music, which was chiefly by Colonna, was excellent in its kind, consisting of fugues well worked, much in Handel's way, with a bold and active base. Some fine effects were produced with the *fortes* and *pianos*, by striking the first note of a bar loud, the rest soft, and by introducing a piece of pathetic for voices only, in the middle of a noisy, full, instrumental chorus.

There was a girl, who sung a solo verse, in the *Credo*, extremely well, in a *mezzo soprano* voice; her shake, and style of singing were good. There were likewise several symphonies for instruments only, composed by M. Hofman, *maestro di capella* of this church, which were well written and well executed, except that the hateful sour organ, poisoned all whenever it played. In the music composed by M. Hofman, though there was great art and contrivance, yet the modulation was natural, and the melody smooth and elegant. . . .

. . . .

M. Gasman is accused by some of want of fire in his theatrical compositions; but the gravity of his style is easily accounted for, by the time and pains he must have bestowed on church music. To aim at equal perfection in both, is trying to serve God and Mammon; and those excellent composers for the church, whose works have survived them, such as Palestrina, Tallis, Birde, Allegri, Benevoli, Colonna, Caldara, Marcello, Lotti, Perti, and Fux, have chiefly confined themselves to the church, style. Alessandro Scarlatti, Handel, Pergolesi, and Jomelli, are exceptions. But, in general, those succeed best in writing for the church, stage, or chamber, who accustom themselves to that particular species of composition only.

I do not call every modern oratorio, mass or motet, *church music:* as the same compositions to different words would do equally well, indeed often better, for the stage. But by *Musica di Chiesa*, properly so called, I mean grave and scientific compositions for voices only, of which the excellence consists more in good harmony, learned modulation, and fugues upon ingenious and sober subjects, than in light airs and turbulent accompaniments.

John Mellen

(1722-1807)

On March 24, 1773, John Mellen, pastor of the Second Church in Lancaster, delivered a sermon at a "Singing Lecture" in Marlborough[1] [Marlboro] in defense of "regular singing." His concern for a higher level of musical worship was shared by many of his contemporaries, especially those who saw value in the singing schools that were being held to acquaint congregations with the fundamentals of note-reading and part-singing. James Lyon and William Billings were among the musicians who favored regular singing, and a number of other ministers supported Mellen in his defense of it. Both Joseph Strong (1729-1803) and Oliver Noble (1734-1792) produced sermons on this subject, but they based their defense of regular singing on scriptural authority to the near exclusion of other arguments. Mellen's discourse also leans heavily on Scripture — most of those passages have been omitted in the following excerpt — but it differs from the others in its greater appeal to logic and in its pleas for music that is suitable to the times in which his audience lived.

Some authors of this period hoped to introduce the devices of secular art music as well. Simeon Jocelin devoted much of the introduction of one of his books [2] to a discussion of graces and ornaments, although few of them are used in the music that follows. Apparently in rebuttal to this secular peril, Oliver Brownson (dates unknown) declined to discuss graces in a publication the following year because "the principal grace that can be used in common schools, is to sing with ease and life, and with hearts deeply affected by a sense of the great truths we utter." [3]

---

[1]Probably the towns are those in Massachusetts.
[2]Simeon Jocelin, *The Chorister's Companion* (New Haven: For Jocelin and Doolittle, [1782]).
[3]Oliver Brownson, *Select Harmony* ([New Haven], 1783), p. 3.

The Service of God[4]

A

GROUND of GLADNESS and SINGING.

Psalm c. ver. 2.

SERVE THE LORD WITH GLADNESS: COME BEFORE HIS

PRESENCE WITH SINGING.

METHINKS, my hearers, this scripture is this day fulfilled in your ears. Do we not serve the Lord with gladness and come before his presence with singing?

This short psalm is a moving exhortation to praise and worship God with chearfulness, grounded upon his greatness, his power and goodness; and wrote in such a strain of pious rapture, as is every way adapted to the noble subject and occasion. The sentiments are lively, sublime and natural, and accompanied with a flow and eloquence that has something in it inimitable. *Make a joyful noise unto the Lord all ye lands. Serve the Lord with gladness. come before his presence with singing. Know ye that the Lord he is GOD. it is he that hath made us and not we ourselves: we are his people and the sheep of his pasture. Enter into his gates with thanksgiving. and into his courts with praise: Be thankful unto him and bless his name. For the Lord is good. his mercy is everlasting. and his truth endureth to all generations.*

We feel a glow of sacred transport at the very rehearsal of this animated poem, and are struck with the *force* of the argument, at the same that we are charmed with the *beauty* of the song. But such poetic compositions set to music, increase the pleasure, and by still further fanning the fire of devotion, serve to waft and elevate the soul to God.

I believe one design of Heaven in intermixing music with devotion, was to recommend religion, and give an air of sprightliness and [illegible] services of the sanctuary.

Very various were the musical instruments of every kind, invented by King *David* and other great masters of song, for celebration of the divine praises, in public worship under the *Jewish* church and dispensation; and very observable the order and

---

[4]Source: John Mellen, *Religion Productive of Music* (Boston: Isaiah Thomas, 1773).

decorum of the instituted band and choir of singers upon their festival, solemn occasions. And in most christian churches some kind of instrumental music is in use, and has been from time immemorial. But of all instruments of music the natural faculty and organ of the human voice is the most noble and excellent. And should that laudable spirit of vocal music that now prevails, be duly encouraged, and those improvements be made in that delightful, sacred art, which present appearances promise, there will be less and less occasion for instrumental aids; and the churches of this land will acquire reputation and honour, will perform the religious music with greater approbation and applause, and soon vie with any churches in the christian world, for the perfection of the *psalmody* that sublime part of devotion, which is the exercise and joy of heaven and earth.

Where church music is performed by instruments there seems to be less ambition to excel in vocal. Our singing women, skilled in the songs of *Zion.* carry the *upper* part of music with a sweetness and pleasure greatly superior to the high-sounding *organ:* And there is less occasion for this instrument upon the *lower* (where, if any where, it might be useful) when great numbers are employed in the sacred song; and seeing nature itself has so ordered it, that much the greater part of masculine voices are accomodated to the grave and sonorous bass.

Serve the Lord with gladness. come before his presence with singing. This chords with the doctrine of St. *James. Is any merry? Let him sing psalms.*

The text harmonizes with nature — chearfulness produces songs — singing is the genuine offspring of a joyous heart.

Such as are unskilled in music, when impressed with agreeable sensations, or a bright scene presents to view, naturally, and as it were involuntarily, burst forth their inward satisfaction and vent their joy in artless singing; which shews the effort of nature to express itself in this way.

But when it can ease and recreate itself, and open a channel for its chearfulness in a way of art and regularity, how pleasing the amusement? And how abundantly are such recompensed for the pains they have taken, or the little time and money they have expended to acquire the knowledge of a liberal, ingenuous art that affords them so much private satisfaction, as well as puts it in their power to give pleasure to others, especially when they come into GOD'S presence with singing, and worship the Lord in the beauties of holiness?

If I can prove, my hearers, that the service of GOD is attended with gladness, and that religion comprehends the grounds and reasons of chearfulness, the other part of the text will appear natural and true, that we should come before GOD'S presence with singing and make a joyful noise unto the rock of our salvation: That we should celebrate the divine praises with a song, and manifest the glad sense we entertain of our own happiness and GOD'S goodness in the regular, well chosen music of the sanctuary.

.   .   .   .

Be glad therefore in the Lord, O ye righteous, and as a natural and fit expression of your joy, and the glad sense you have of the reasonableness of religion and the excellency and advantageousness of GOD'S service, and agreeable to the requirement in the text, *Come before his presence with singing.*

Now in order to this, my brethren, you are sensible several things are necessary. We should be poorly equipped for coming into God's presence with singing, without something properly prepared to be sung, without a tune previously composed to sing it in, without art and skill in the music to be performed, without suitable persons employed and leading in the several parts of harmony, and regular disposition of things in order to [exercise] social praise and singing in concert. Without these things, a number, even of the devoutest christians, assembled for the divine praise, would resemble the broken church of *Corinth.* in that state of irregularity and disorder, when the Apostle asks them, if any come into your assemblies, under these circumstances, *will they not say that they are mad? How is it then, brethren? When ye come together every one of you hath a psalm, hath a doctrine, hath a tongue, hath a revelation. Let all things be done to edifying. For GOD is not the author of confusion but of peace, as in all the churches of the Saints.*

Any one may imagine to himself the disturbance and jargon that must be occasioned by such a plurality and diversity of songs, tunes and unskilful voices, all in motion at once, interfering, inconsistent and discordant!

In the first place therefore, when we come before GOD'S presence with singing, we must be united in a *song.* The whole church, assembly, or band of social worshippers must conform themselves to the portion proposed to be sung, or the words set to music.

These are psalms, hymns and spiritual songs, parcelled out by the masters of our religious assemblies, suitable to times, occasions and circumstances. This requires some judgment, attention and discretion, in such as from time to time, propose and deal out the songs of *Zion*.

And happy it is for the christian world that they are supplied with such a rich variety of noble compositions of this kind, upon all divine subjects, founded upon the holy scriptures, and especially adapted to the christian age and gospel day.

The book of psalms is a most excellent collection of worthy and sublime songs. But methinks such christians deprive themselves of a great pleasure and advantage, who confine themselves to the poetical compositions of those ancient ages and dispensations, less suitable in general, to the free and benevolent spirit of christianity, when we abound so much with spiritual songs and hymns, in the New-Testament taste, and done by so many pious and able hands. The psalms of *David*, the sweet singer of *Israel*, ought surely never to be neglected, undervalued or disused. But why should gospel sonnets be wholly omitted by christians, who are required to cultivate the evangelical rather than the legal spirit? A late pious songster who has obliged the christian world with the largest number of devotional and scriptural hymns, is pleased to say, "While we sing the praises of GOD in his church, we are employed in that part of worship which of all others is nearest a-kin to heaven; and it is pity, that this of all others should be performed the worst upon earth. The gospel brings us nearer to the heavenly state than all the former dispensations of GOD amongst men: And in these last days of the gospel we are brought almost within sight of the kingdom of our LORD; yet we are very much unacquainted with the songs of the *New-Jerusalem*, and unpractised in the work of praise.

"To see the dull indifference, the negligent and the thoughtless air that sits upon the faces of a whole assembly, while the psalm is on their lips, might tempt even a charitable observer to suspect the fervency of inward religion. Of all our religious solemnities psalmody is the most unhappily managed: That very action which should elevate us to the most delightful and divine sensations doth not only flat our devotions, but too often awakens our regret, and touches all the springs of uneasiness within us.

"I have been long convinced (he goes on) that one great occasion of this evil arises from the matter and words to which we confine all our songs. Some of them are almost opposite to the spirit of the gospel: Many of them foreign to the state of the *New-Testament*, and widely different from the present circumstances of christians. Hence it comes to pass, that when spiritual affections

are excited in us, and our souls are raised a little above this earth
in the beginning of a psalm we are checked on a sudden in our
ascent towards heaven, by some expressions that are more suited to
the days of *carnal ordinances.* and fit only to be sung in the worldly
sanctuary. Thus by keeping too close to *David* in the house of
GOD, the veil of *Moses* is thrown over our hearts. While we are
kindling into divine love, by the meditations of the loving
kindness of GOD, and the multitude of his tender mercies, within
a few verses some dreadful curse against men is proposed to our
lips, &c."

.   .   .   .

But it is not only necessary when we come before GOD'S
presence with singing, that we bring a *song and a tune*—we must
also bring *art* and *skill* in psalmody, and be able to sing the songs
of the Lord according to rule and order, so as to make sweet and
agreeable harmony, and not discord and confusion. What horrid jar
and grating dissonance, must be the consequence of a large
number of voices lifted up on high without art or regularity, or
conformity to time or tune? What a clash of unharmonious
sounds, and notes interfering and disgustful! Was every one to
follow his artless fancy in forming sounds at pleasure, of any
length or distance, the discord must be dreadful!

Such a diversity of accidental tunes, and murdered sounds,
would be inconceivably more shocking than a plurality of songs
and psalms, regularly sung to the same tune. He that so wisely
constructed the delicate and wonderful organ of the ear, never
designed it should be prostituted to such a barbarous use; — Nor
did heaven endow us with the pleasing powers of harmony, above
the brutes, that we should neglect the gift of GOD that is in us,
and come before his presence with confused noise of artless
sounds, like the congregated flocks, and lowing herds.

But it must be an affront to common sense and decency, to
labour the argument in favour of *art* and *rule.* either in composing
or performing music. They are so plainly necessary, that we now
stand amazed at the opposition once made to what was called the
regular way of singing. It is beyond all account, that towns and
churches should have suffered themselves to be broken and divided
on such a point as this! And will not children yet unborn, be
struck hereafter with equal astonishment, at the offence taken by
some few, at the present reformation in singing, and the happy
revival of the spirit of music? Will it not appear wonderful, that

such *discord* should spring from *harmony*, and that societies should again a second time suffer themselves to be rent in pieces, by an eager, violent contention about little formalities and customs, *harmless* in themselves, and *useful* in the work of praise? Rule and measure is allowed and thought necessary in all other arts, and why not in the noble science of music and psalmody? In nothing are they more necessary. Without them no piece of music could be constructed; or performed to edification, or without the utmost confusion, when made. *Epicurus's*, stragling atoms might as well form by accident such a regular, harmonious world as this, as that an agreeable, concordant piece of music should be performed, in concert and in all its parts, by the casual artless sound of notes, without any previous disposition, or knowledge and observance of tune and measure. Methodical books might as well be made, and a syllogistic dispute be carried on, by an accidental shuffle of a sufficient number of the letters of the alphabet, as that real music and harmony, should be the offspring of ignorance and undesigning chance. Moreover, when we come before GOD'S presence with singing, there must be some to *govern the music*, to appoint the tune, and give the pitch, within the compass of the voice, in all the parts; which requires the niceness of judgment, and is difficult, in many cases to be done, without that help of art, now discovered, which is much the same to the voice that glasses are to the eyes. There must be some to take the several parts, and lead upon them — and a certain disposition and placing of those, who, more especially are over the song, may be convenient, to unite the *parts* and give them strength, in some *common centre*, that each may be distinguished, and rightly balanced, and so that those at greater distance may join their voices where it suits them, or if they have skill, upon the part that needs them most. Thus *David* appointed a large number that "were instructed in the songs of the Lord, even all that were *cunning*."[a] artists and proficients in music. Such *David* set over the service of song in the house of the Lord.[b] *And moreover the singers, the sons of Asaph were IN THEIR PLACE, according to the commandment of David*.[c] And we are told particularly how they sung in concert and unison, 2 Cron.v.13. *And it came to pass, as the trumpeters and singers were as one, to make one sound to be heard, in praising and thanking the Lord: and when they lift up their voice with the trumpets and cymbals and*

---

[a] 1 Cron.xxv.7.
[b] vi.31.
[c] 2 Cron.xxxv.15.

instruments of music, and praised the Lord, saying, for he is good, for his mercy endureth forever: that then the house was filled with a cloud, even the house of the Lord. Thus the GOD of *Israel* manifested his acceptance of their regular, melodious praise and thanksgiving. But will he accept our unharmonious sounds and grating discords, if we slothfully neglect to acquire, or encourage, that art and skill he has given us, to render our songs sweet and concordant?

I know it is the heart that is chiefly to be regarded; and *there* we should especially endeavour to make melody to the Lord. But we must sing with the understanding as well as heart. The rule and art of singing, is no hindrance to the piety and devotion of it. Such men argue strangely, as contend that in order to please GOD, we must sing so as to offend men. It becomes us to serve GOD with our best.

Samuel Arnold

(1740-1802)

Interest in the history and traditions of English cathedral music ran high in the second half of the eighteenth century. William Boyce (1710-1779) published a three-volume set of Services and anthems during the years 1760-78, Arnold followed with his four volumes (one of which contained organ parts for the works printed for voices only in the other three), and John Page (1760-1812) published his three volumes entitled *Harmonia Sacra* in 1800. Together with *The First Book of Selected Church Music* (1641) by John Barnard (dates unknown) and Thomas Tudway's (1650-1726) six volumes of manuscript, "A Collection of the Most Celebrated Services and Anthems . . ." (British Museum MSS Harley 7337-7342), much of the music for a history of Anglican musical practice, at least of the cathedral practice, is presented by these men. In each case, the purpose of the set was to present the best works in readily available form for performance, or to retrieve them from possible oblivion as important documents in the nation's musical heritage.

Preface to Cathedral Music [1]

As the late Doctor Boyce lived only to compleat Three Volumes of Cathedral Musick, and as many of the Valuable Works of the English Composers, (who were so eminent in that stile of writing) which he had not room to insert in his work, appear to me to be worthy of preservation; I have undertaken a Supplement to it, trusting it will not be unacceptable to the remaining few, who have judgment to taste their sublimities, and liberality enough to encourage it.

Indeed I am well aware that the encouragement will not be great, as it is not the fashion to study Church, so much as secular Musick; and if the Cathedral and Churches in England, Scotland, Ireland and Wales, where Choir Service is performed (and for whose use this work was principally intended) do not encourage it,

[1]Source: Samuel Arnold (ed.), *Cathedral Music* . . . (4 vols.; London: For the editor, 1790), I, 5.

94

the time may come, when this sublime, tho' much neglected stile
of Composition (so well understood by our forefathers) will be
totally lost in this Kingdom.

In order to render this work as useful and easy as the nature of
it will admit, I have removed the C, Cliff from the Treble parts,
and substituted the G, Cliff, and at the request of many
Gentlemen in the profession, I have printed a separate part for the
Organ to every Service and Anthem &c. the reason for which will
appear too obvious to point out.

Doctor Boyce remarks in his Preface, "that no person employed
to copy Church Musick can afford to provide good paper, and
write what is here contained in a page at the price those pages are
sold for, which is less than seven farthings each; this must
undoubtedly be the cheapest, and most eligible way of purchasing
Books for the above mentioned purpose," to which, I beg leave to
remark, that the work I have undertaken, will be deliverd to
Subscribers at a trifle more than Four Farthings a page: and, if (in
the words of my worthy predecessor) there should arise to me any
further benefit than the reputation of perpetuating those valuable
remains of my ingenious countrymen, it will be more than I
expect.

S. Arnold

Nov.r 1.st 1790
N.º 480 Strand.

Richard Eastcott

(1740-1828)

One of the most violent attacks against imitative counterpoint in church music was launched by Richard Eastcott, a clergyman who wrote about church music. He was a composer of some ability, but his extant works are secular, so it is not known whether he followed his own advice in religious composition. His *Sketches of the Origin, Progress and Effects of Music* was so well received that a second edition had to be prepared the same year the first appeared. The only chapter that has any value now is the one quoted here. The age-old problem of the function of music in the church service is discussed, especially from the standpoint of the balance of importance between text and music. In Eastcott's opinion, text must ever emerge victorious in church, especially as it is scriptural, and its clarity must remain unimpaired. Without ever making a direct statement to that effect, he makes clear the fact that the earlier injunctions against melismatic treatment have been discarded in many instances, and his comments about choirs and the singers therein make one wonder if there was no longer a creditable choral group in all of England.

Chap. XII.[1]

Of the use and abuse of Church Music

"I will sing with the spirit, and I will sing with the understanding also."

St. Paul.

The general use of music, in almost all places of public worship, from the earliest times to this day, shews that although mankind, in the several ages of the world, have differed widely on their religious opinions, yet they have all agreed that music is capable of animating the affections, of creating sublime ideas, and the most holy aspirations. The prophets from *Moses to Malachi*, adapted their

---

[1]Richard Eastcott, *Sketches of the Origin, Progress and Effects of Music, with an Account of the Ancient Bards and Minstrels* (2nd ed.; Bath: S. Hazard, 1793), pp. 169-94.

96

inspired compositions to music, and the service of the *Temple* required the union of voice, and instruments to make it perfect and complete.

We have the example of Christ, under the dispensation of the gospel, to authorize and sanction its use in the *christian church*, and from the constant practice of it among the primitive christians, we may fairly conclude, that they considered it as essentially necessary in their devotional exercises, and conformable to the practice of those blessed and exalted beings, who form the ministry of the triumphant church in heaven. We have indisputable testimony of the early use of hymns among christians, even before churches were built, or the christian religion was established by law.

St. Ambrose. St. Augustine. St. Gregory. St. Basil. St. Chrysostom. St. Jerome. &c. &c. sanctioned and cultivated sacred music. *St. Ambrose, bishop of Milan, and St. Hilary, bishop of Poitiers,* composed sacred hymns. St. Ambrose and St. Gregory, are recorded not only as fathers of the church, but of church music. The Ambrosian and the Gregorian chants, I apprehend, are still in use, in the Roman church.

Music, in the early ages of christianity, is said to have drawn the Gentiles into the church through novelty, and we are told, that they were so captivated, and liked its ceremonies so well, that many of them were baptized, before they left the congregation. Dr. Burney says, "The generality of our parochial music is more likely to drive christians out of the church, than draw pagans into it." A more just observation surely was never made.

It is a lamentable truth, that the general manner of performing parochial music, is become an object of disgust, instead of rational delight, founded upon religious edification. Psalmody, in its present state, serves only to excite contempt and to invite ridicule. The jargon of heterogeneous sounds, introduced of late into our churches, serve to drown devotion in the most clamorous outcries. A sunday's exhibition may give a congregation an idea of Bartholomew fair, or Smithfield market; it may paint to their minds the confusion of tongues, at the building of the tower of Babel, or the tremendous sounds of the rams-horns and the shouting of the people before the walls of Jericho: but as well may we expect the piety of the rational christian to be called forth, and his affections to be engaged in praise and thanksgiving, in the midst of the like scenes, I have just mentioned, as in our churches, during the indecent anticks and indecorous noise of those celebrated performers, who compose a country choir.

Many of the old psalm tunes, which were introduced into our

churches soon after the reformation and some of the modern ones,
composed by approved masters, are exceedingly well calculated to
inspire devotion and to elevate the soul; they are, in general,
solemn and expressive, easily to be acquired, and their melodies are
so pleasing and simple, that, when once learnt, it will be very
difficult to forget them.

Had I the regulation of the musical department of a parochial
church, where there is no organ, I would never permit any tune to
be introduced, consisting of more than two parts. As to fugue
tunes, I would immediately discard them. By these means, the
congregation would not be precluded from a part of the service in
which it is the duty of *all* who are capable, to join.

The present worthy *bishop of London*, in his excellent charge to
his clergy, at his primary visitation, takes particular notice of the
indecent manner, in which parochial music is generally performed,
and strongly recommends this divine service to the particular
attention of his clergy, as standing in need of great reformation.

The ignorance frequently displayed in the selection of the
words,[a] as well as in the choice of those barbarous tunes in
common use, make it necessary that a selection of certain portions
of the psalms, adapted to proper melodies, should be undertaken
by approved persons; *and that the tunes, as well as the words, should be
sanctioned by royal authority. Were a committee to be appointed for this
purpose, consisting of the subdean, two of the priests in ordinary, and the
two organists of the royal chapel of St. James, under the inspection of the
dean, there can be no doubt, but this useful and necessary work would soon
be completed in the most judicious, and correct manner.* These gentlemen,
although members of cathedral churches, are likewise, I apprehend,
parochial clergymen, and parochial organists. This scheme, in my
humble opinion, is not impracticable, and were any thing like it
ever to be adopted, I would, with great deference, advise that the
number of tunes sanctioned, should not exceed thirty six, which
supposing six to be used each sunday, would come round in
rotation every six weeks. This number, judiciously selected, would
be sufficient for all the purposes of supplication, praise, and
thanksgiving, and our church would have a sublime and rational
service, performed by a sober and reasonable congregation. These
hints are intended as the mere outlines of a plan, which I shall be
happy to see improved and brought to perfection by persons of

---

[a] The version of the psalms by *Tate and Brady*, is in general much better calculated for music, than
that of *Sternhold and Hopkins*, but Dr. Merrick's (which cannot be used in our churches because not
privileged by royal authority) is infinitely superior to either of them.

ability and judgment.

It may not be amiss to hint, that music does not consist in the quantity of tone produced, but in the quality; in other words, that it does not consist in noise, as too many imagine, for if we may judge from observation, the most vociferous singer is generally considered the most useful, although he has not a single musical idea, and can scarcely distinguish one tone from another. If it should be advanced, that it is impossible, to regulate a great number of mixed voices, and to keep them within proper bounds, so as to produce an even and pleasing volume of sound, I answer that this effect is annually produced by the greatest part of five thousand *charity children* singing together, at their general assembly at *St. Paul's*. The celebrated *Doctor Hayden*. declared lately to a friend of mine, that the strongest musical impression he had ever received, was made on him by these children, singing a psalm to a plain melody, which he said affected him so powerfully, that he was confident he should remember it to his latest hour. Indeed the order and regularity observed, and the ideas of compassion and benevolence naturally excited in the mind, at the sight of such a delightful spectacle as this assembly, must ever engage the attention of the humane, and fill the heart of the beneficent with unspeakable satisfaction. But to return. There are many indecencies and inconveniencies, which attend the present mode of conducting parochial psalmody, sufficient, each of them, to create a desire in every serious christian to lend his assistance to check evils, which every one complains of, and which are increasing to a shameful degree. One among the catalogue is, that the singers belonging to many of our parochial churches, attend very little to any other part of the service, but, between the psalms, are continually talking and turning over the leaves of their anthem books, and from the time they come into church, 'till they leave it, they carelessly pass over every other part of their duty, and seem to consider the prayers and sermon as matters of little consequence, and not worthy their attention. There is another evil, which I shall point out, and which may easily be removed: which is, the mis-apprehensions, which frequently happen in those churches, where there is an organ, between the clerk and the organist. I know several parish churches, where violent altercations have taken place between these two officers of the church, even during divine service; and the frequent messages, sent from one to the other, have often created the greatest confusion. I was lately present at a scene of this kind, which happened in a parish church within a few miles of London. The clerk gave out the psalm, and the organist played *a tune* once

over, and then stopped for the clerk to read the first sentence of
the psalm as usual; instead of which the clerk called out, "that's
not the tune which was sent up Mr._____," here a considerable
pause took place, when finding no notice was taken by the
organist, he hollowed out again in a louder tone of voice, "play
Islington tune," here a second pause took place, while I suppose
the organist was finding the tune required, however he soon found
it and all went on tolerably well. Why not settle what psalms are
to be performed before the service begins? the consultation would
not take two minutes, and would prevent every kind of mistake
and confusion.

I wish every parochial church possessed a good organ, played by
an attentive and skilful organist, but as the generality of country
parishes are not of ability to purchase an organ and to make a
proper provision for an organist, very good effects may be
produced by a number of *well regulated voices*. even without this
assistance. The methods to produce these desirable effects are, to
dissolve all *select bands*. to admonish the individuals, who composed
them, to be amenable, and to consider, that it is the Almighty and
Eternal God whose praises *all* meet to celebrate; to recommend a
strict attention to the plainest melodies, and to endeavour to
convince those, who may signify an intention of joining in this
service, that no voice ought to be distinctly heard above the rest,
but that a certain medium of sound should be strictly attended to,
so that all the different tones may meet in one degree of
temperature and produce a pleasing and heavenly agreement. I am
sensible a great deal may be done with very little difficulty, if
people will carefully observe these rules, instead of obstinately
persisting in those irreverent and disgusting methods, which have
brought our parochial music into universal contempt.

There is one great advantage, which plain melodies have over
complex tunes, which is, that they require no other qualifications
in the performers, than a tolerable voice, and a good ear. A person
may be totally ignorant of the science of music, and yet be able to
sing these tunes with great correctness. The *charity children*. at
their general assembly, are one instance of this truth, and the
methodists and other *dissenting congregations*. in London, Bath, and
elsewhere, of whom but few of the individuals, I believe, even
know their notes, almost universally excel in performing hymns
and common psalm tunes; by alloting a small portion of their
time to practice, they have arrived to a certain point of excellency,
scarcely known in any of our churches; they consider this part of
the service with that attention it deserves, and do all in their

power to perform it with suitable devotion, and the effect arising from the union of their voices, all who have ever heard, must pronounce delightful.

It has been said, and I believe with great truth, that many of the converts among the methodists have declared that the singing was their primary attraction. If we are sensible of the great efficacy of this system of the methodists in gaining proselytes, surely there can be no reason, why the established church and other places of worship should not adopt it. Every warrantable method it is undoubtedly, our duty most strenuously to pursue; by first warming the affections, we shall afterwards have an opportunity of convincing the understanding; and if we are happy enough to make a convert, it matters but little, whether the primary attraction was sound or sense, provided we retain him by producing irrefragable arguments in favour of the faith he hath embraced.

I shall now take the liberty to make a few observations on the nature and tendency of the compositions commonly in use in our cathedrals, and the general manner of performing them. In cathedrals, the full services and anthems are frequently composed of four parts: each part ought to produce such an even proportion of sound, that no one part should be particularly heard: instead of which, it is not uncommon to hear seven or eight boys, singing the treble part as loud as they can bawl, while each of the other three parts, are supported by one, or two voices at the most. By this means the composer's intentions are frustrated, and all ideas of devotion in the congregation are entirely destroyed. To produce a proper effect, an equal number of voices, producing an equal quantity of tone, ought to support each part, by which all the parts would be so blended together, as to appear one uniform body of sound.

On reading the *Te-Deum*. the ideas of *praise. adoration* and *petition*. alternately fill the mind, but as it is set by some of the *old masters*. it is rendered incapable of creating a single idea of praise, adoration, or petition; the whole is conveyed in one dull tune from the beginning to the end, without the least variation, and the same notes would equally as well express the words of an act of parliament. Some of our *modern composers*. in order to correct the faults of the ancients, have run into the contrary extreme, they have set the *Te-Deum* in such a familiar stile, that the dignity of the subject is degraded by the levity of the composition: however, it must be allowed that greater regard has been paid to measure, stops, and expression, by the moderns, than by the ancients, and that their compositions, for the most part, possess more melody.

As to *solo anthems*, the generality of them are, in my opinion, destructive of devotion, they are calculated to shew the abilities of the singer, and the extravagant flights of the composer, but nothing farther. The running long divisions of notes upon the most unemphatic words, which is frequently the case, breaks the connection of every sentence thus abused, and leaves the congregation destitute of a single idea of piety or "edification unto godliness." In those anthems, which are composed of three or four parts, fugue tunes are often introduced, which, as musical compositions, are in many instances very ingenious, but whenever they are connected with poetry, they create such manifest confusion, that the sense of the poetry is swallowed up in the reiterated sounds of the music. To point out the absurdity of this stile of composition, I will mention two anthems *only*, which will be sufficient to convince any person, although totally unacquainted with music, of the impropriety of its being permitted to make a part of the service of the church. I will beg the reader's attention for a moment to a celebrated and well known anthem, which begins with the verse of the 116th psalm, "I am well pleased, &c. &c." the original music is by *Carrissini*, and was adapted to the words of this psalm by the late learned *Dr. Aldrich*, dean of Christ church, who added some ingenious and useful compositions of his own to the stock of our cathedral music. The eighth verse of this psalm is employed in a fugue, composed for three voices, I will write a few of the words down as they are set, and consequently sung.

1st Voice.

——————————————For he hath deliver'd my soul, my soul from death, and

2d Voice.

For he hath deliver'd my soul, my soul from death, mine eyes from tears, and

3d Voice.

——————For he hath deliver'd my soul, my soul from death, my feet——————

No three persons can possibly sing or read these words, as I have written them, which is exactly as they stand in the composition, without destroying the sense totally. The eye of the reader will instantly perceive how miserably these words are jumbled together, let him only look to the four last words of each line, and he will find that while the first person is singing, "my soul from death," the second is singing, "mine eyes from tears," and the third, "from death my feet," and all these words beat up together, meet the ears of the congregation at the same time. Were the *Lord's prayer. the apostles' creed.* and the *exhortation* to be performed in the same manner, the whole, to a person unacquainted with music would be just as intelligible. I will now write down the same words as it appears to me, they ought to be set, in order to preserve the sense.

1st Voice.
For he hath deliver'd my soul from death, mine eyes from tears, and

2d Voice.
For he hath deliver'd my soul from death, mine eyes from tears, and

3d Voice.
For he hath deliver'd my soul from death, mine eyes from tears, and

The reader will see, in a moment, that if three persons sing the words as I have now written them, each person will express the same word at the same time, by which means the sense will be preserved.

I shall now introduce to your notice an anthem, composed by Orlando Gibbons, for six voices and intended for a full choir. It is allowed to be a very ingenious composition. The words are taken from the 24th psalm, beginning with the 7th verse. I shall beg the reader to get six persons to read the words as written on the other side, previous to which, I must request him to desire each person to set off according to the distances marked, which, if all strictly attend to, must produce the following effects. — When the first person pronounces the word *up.* the second person will pronounce the word *lift.* and when the third person begins the sentence, the following words will be pronounced together.

$$\left\{ \begin{array}{c} \text{Lift} \\ \text{heads} \\ \text{your} \end{array} \right\}$$

Through the whole of this anthem there is a race kept up between six voices, who continually justle each other to the very last note.

The words as they are set to music by
Orlando Gibbons

1st. Voice.

Lift up your heads O————————ye gates, ————Lift up your heads

2d Voice.

————Lift up——your heads,———Lift up your heads,———Lift up your heads

3d Voice.

————————————Lift up,———Lift up your heads, ————————————

4th Voice.

————————————Lift up————————————your heads,————————

5th Voice.

————————————————————Lift up your heads O————

6th Voice.

————————————————————————Lift up————

There is nothing, however absurd, but what custom is capable of reconciling. Some of our venerable old choir-men, from long use, esteem this anthem with a degree of enthusiasm, not considering, that, though the words and music are, each in their separate state, allowed to be most excellent compositions, yet, as they are here joined together, they form a most unnatural connection.—In *Dr. Wharton's history of English poetry*. vol. 3. It is recorded that *Dr. Christopher Tye, musical preceptor to prince Edward.*[b] *translated the first fourteen chapters of the acts of the apostles into english metre, and set them to music for the service of the royal chapels.* This work was printed in 1553, and was in use a short time, but the impropriety of the design, and the impotency of the execution, rendered it preposterous and exceptionable, in the opinion of men of understanding, and the work was consigned to oblivion." A stranger idea surely never entered the head of man, than to suppose by such a manifest incongruity, he could elevate the soul in the sacred hours of devotion. We may judge of the degree of

---

bEdward VI. I have seen the same accounts in other authors.

elevation, the Doctor's soul was arrived at, by the following lines, which make part of his dedication to the king's most excellent majesty.

"Your grace may *note* from tyme to tyme,
That some doth undertake
Upon the psalms to write in ryme,
The verse pleasant to make:

And last of all, I your poor man,
Whose doings are *full base.*
Yet glad to do the best I can
To give unto your grace."

It is a well known truth, that the generality of people are more satisfied with having their ears tickled, than they are to have their minds informed, or their hearts affected. Composers therefore consider, that if they do not comply with the corrupt taste of the age in which they live, they stand little chance either of fame or profit; but I will with great humility, recommend all composers, who are employed in the service of the Temple, to have the following scriptural aphorism, written in large characters, placed over the instrument they commonly use, when they compose sacred music. *"Whatsoever ye do. do it unto the Lord. and he will prosper the work of your hands."*

Religion is the most delightful field for the meditation of a musical composer. In different parts of holy writ, particularly the psalms, he will find all the variety of subjects, which music can express, and if he has a taste for sublime poetry, his heart will be warmed with devout enthusiasm. *Marcello. a noble Venetian.* has availed himself of this divine treasure, and has so happily adapted his music to the words of a considerable number of the psalms, that the dignity and sublimity of every sentence, seem to receive additional energy from the skill of the composer.

Sacred music. as we have seen, can boast the highest antiquity, it has claimed a place in the religious institutions almost of every nation. *The Grecians and the Romans* among the heathens, and *the Jews* and *Christians* of the sacred world, although they disagreed in all other parts of their œconomy, did unanimously agree in this. It is therefore devoutly to be wished, that christians of every denomination would seriously attend to this exalted service, and consider it as a religious duty; if it is not performed with decency and reverential awe, it cannot be an acceptable service to the

Almighty, in whose presence we are told, "Is the fulness of joy and pleasures for evermore." *The celestial hierarchies,* and the innumerable *hosts of angels* are represented, as perpetually surrounding the throne of God, singing hymns of praise, and if we believe the descriptions of heaven in holy scripture, we must conclude, that this will make part of the happiness of the blessed hereafter, in the glorious mansions of eternal bliss. Let us then, by joining in the songs of Sion in the church militant here on earth, prepare ourselves for joining with angels in the church triumphant in heaven, where "after this world shall be no more, and Christ shall have delivered up the kingdom to God even the Father," all nations, kindred, and people shall as with one voice proclaim, "Blessing, and glory, and wisdom, and thanksgiving, and honour, and might, be unto our God for ever and ever. Amen." [c]

---

[c] Vide, Dr. Brown's dissertation on the union of poetry and music. Dr. Vincent on parochial music. Dr. Watts's preface to his translation of the psalms. Dr. Burney's history of music, vol. 3, p. 60. Spectator, No. 405, 580, 630.

William Billings

(1746-1800)

The first half of the eighteenth century had already seen a conflict between the adherents to the old style of singing that depended on oral tradition and the proponents of "regular singing," *i.e.*, according to the printed page. Differences arose between rural and urban groups; between tutored and untutored; between congregations that favored "lining-out" of the tune by a deacon and those that desired accuracy and continuity in the singing. The cause of regular singing was advanced by the great number of tunebooks that began to appear in New England in the latter half of the century. Their usefulness, in turn, was increased by the wide acceptance of the singing schools, where people gathered to learn regular singing and simple music theory, often receiving their instruction from the compiler of the tunebook himself.

William Billings was one of the best known of the composer-compilers. Self-taught in music, as many of his fellows were, he brought to American church music a vigor that is unparalleled by his better educated competitors. In his theoretical introduction to *The Continental Harmony*. he presented a complete course of music study in eight lessons, and followed it with a dialogue that reviews the principal sections. The extract that follows is taken from the dialogue.

Extract from The Continental Harmony[1]

A COMMENTARY . . . by way of DIALOGUE, between MASTER and SCHOLAR

. . . .

Scholar.   Sir, I should be glad to know which key you think is best; the flat, or the sharp key?[2]

Master.   I believe your question would puzzle the greatest

---

[1]Source: William Billings, *The Continental Harmony* . . . (Boston: Isaiah Thomas and Ebenezer T. Andrews, 1794), pp. xxi-xxiii. There is a facsimile edition with Introduction by Hans Nathan (Cambridge, Mass.: The Belknap Press of Harvard University Press, 1961).

[2]*i.e.*. major and minor.

philosopher, or practitioner, upon earth; for there are so many excellent pieces on each key, that we are apt to fall in with a certain man, who heard two very eminent lawyers plead in opposition to each other; after the first had done speaking, the man was so charmed with his eloquence and oratory, that he thought it would be an idle (as well as a rash) attempt for any one to gainsay, or contradict him; but when he had heard the second, he said, that his reasons were so nervous and weighty, he was about to give him the preference; upon which the first made so forcible a reply, that the man knew not what to say, at last he concluded they were both best. Similar to this, let us suppose ourselves to be auditors to a company of musicians; how enraptured should we be to hear the sharp key, express itself in such lofty and majestic strains as these! *O come let us sing unto the Lord. let us make a joyful noise. to the rock of our salvation: let us come before his presence with thanksgiving. and make a joyful noise unto him with psalms. Sing unto the Lord all the earth. make a loud noise. rejoice and sing praise!* Do I hear the voice of men or angels! surely such angelic sounds cannot proceed from the mouths of sinful mortals: but while we are yet warm with the thought, and ravished with the sound, the musicians change their tone, and the flat[a] key utters itself in strains so moving, and pathetic, that it seems at least to command our attention to such mournful sounds as these: *Hear my prayer O Lord. give ear to my supplication. hear me speedily: O Lord my spirit faileth. hide not thy face from me: O my God. my soul is cast down within me. Have pity upon me. O ye my friends. for the hand of God hath touched me.* O how these sounds thrill through my soul! how agreeably they affect my nerves! how soft, how sweet, how soothing! methinks these sounds are more expressive than the other, for they affect us both with pleasure and pain, but the *pleasure* is so great it makes even *pain* to be pleasant, so that for the sake of the pleasure, I could forever bear that pain. But hark! what shout is that? It seems the sharp key is again upon the wing towards heaven; jealous, perhaps, that we pay too much deference to his rival: he not only desires, but *commands* us to join in such exalted strains at these. *Rejoice in the Lord. and again I say. rejoice. O*

---

[a] I take this opportunity to make this remark, viz. the impropriety of setting a *Hallelujah* in a flat key; the reader may observe, that the import of the word is, *Praise ye the Lord.*— Query, is it not very inconsistent to praise the Lord, in tones which are plaintive and prayerful? for certainly the words and the music, must contradict each other. N.B. This errour I confess myself guilty of in a former publication, but upon more mature reflection, I heartily wish it were in my power to erase it.

*clap your hands all ye people. shout unto God with the voice of triumph:
God is gone up with a shout. the Lord with the sound of a trumpet: sing
praises to God. sing praises. sing praises unto our King. sing praises.*
What an ecstacy of joy may we suppose the Royal Author to be in
when he composed this Psalm of praise! perhaps it might be some
such strain as this, that expelled the evil spirit, and I wish it
might expel some of the *evil spirits* in these days, who are averse to
hearing God's praises sung, in such a manner as the Psalmist has
here pointed out: but I would refer such persons to King David,
for their character, who says, *they are like the deaf adder. who stoppeth
her ear. and will not hearken to the voice of charmers. charming never so
wisely.* But to return, you see the extreme difficulty, and almost
impossibility of giving the preference to either of these keys, both
of which are so agreeable to our natures, and are so excellent that
they seem to excel each other;[b] for when we are just about to
declare ourselves in favour of one, the other comes and pleads its
own cause so powerfully upon our nerves, that it not only staggers,
but sometimes sets us quite beside our purpose; for the one is so
sublime, so grand, and so majestic,[c] the other, so soft, so soothing,
so pathetic; in fact, the key which comes last seems to be the best,
and generally leaves the greatest impression. History gives us an
account very similar to this in the Life of Alexander the Great,
viz. that while he was sitting at table (calmly and quietly) his
musician would strike a majestic strain on the sharp key, sounding
to arms. to arms. to arms. in such animating and commanding
sounds, that the king being filled with martial rage, would start
from table, draw his sword, and be just about to sally forth, in
order to slay his enemies, when none were near him; but even
while martial fury had the ascendency over reason, the musicians
would change the key, and play such moving and melting airs;
viz. *Darius is fall'n. fall'n. fall'n.* that the king (being melted into
pity) would let his sword drop out of his hand, sit down and weep
heartily for him, whose destruction he had been always seeking,
and whose ruin he had but just accomplished. For my own
curiosity I have been very critical in my observations, and very

---

b It is probable that at the first glance, this may appear inconsistent, viz. that any two things opposed
should be said to excel each other; but I presume (upon second thought) all who are judges of music
will allow that the sharp and the flat key are so excellent each in its own way, that considering them in
this light, though so different, they may (without any impropriety) be said to excel each other.
c I think it may not be amiss to rank the sharp key (by reason of its majesty and grandeur) in the
masculine, and flat key (by reason of its softness and effeminacy) in the feminine gender; and all indifferent pieces, which are of no force in either key, may (with contempt) be ranked in the neuter.

industrious in my inquiries, and I find that most men who are
lovers of music, are affected in the same manner (though not often
to such a degree) as Alexander was; but at the same time, if all,
who are lovers of music, were to decide the point by vote, I am
positive the flat key would have the preference by a great
majority.

THE NINETEENTH CENTURY

Ludwig van Beethoven

(1770-1827)

The conflict between man's ideals and his physical needs is demonstrated in excerpts from Beethoven's letters relating to his *Missa Solemnis*, a work generally accepted without dispute as a meaningful religious expression in music. Still, Beethoven's need for money — as a man of modest means in an inflationary age — is reflected in his efforts to obtain exposure for his piece, a suitable sum for his labors, and, as a further effort, his willingness to compromise the continuity, organization, and perhaps even the function, of his Mass in order to realize some substantial income from the piece. The excerpts are only a part of his correspondence on this matter during a period of more than a year and a half. Of the men to whom he addressed his problems, the three represented here are the most significant. Carl Friedrich Zelter (1758-1832) was connected with the Berlin Singakademie, and was virtual dictator of its policies. Johann Joseph Rudolph, Archduke of Austria (1788-1831), was Beethoven's patron, and it was for his installation as Archbishop of Olomouc in 1820 that Beethoven intended to have the Mass finished. The work was completed nearly two years later. Hans Georg Nägeli (1773-1836) was a Swiss music publisher with whom Beethoven had previously done business. The contents and tone of the various excerpts clearly show the way Beethoven hoped to involve these three, among others, in making his Mass a profitable venture.

To Zelter.[1]

Vienna, Feb. 8, 1823.

My Brave Colleague in Art,

I write, having a favour to ask of you, for we are now so distant from each other that we can no longer converse together, and, indeed, unhappily, we can seldom write either. I have written a grand Mass, which might also be given as an Oratorio (for the benefit of the poor, a good established custom here). I do not wish to publish it in the usual way, but to dispose of it to some of the

[1]Source, *Beethoven's Letters (1790-1826)*, trans. by Lady Wallace (2 vols., London: Longmans, Green, and Co., 1866), II, 101-02.

112

leading courts alone. I ask fifty ducats for it. No copies are to be sold except those subscribed for, so that the Mass will be, as it were, in manuscript, but there must be a fair number of subscribers, if any profit is to accrue to the author. I have made an application to the Prussian embassy here, to know if the King of Prussia would vouchsafe to take a copy, and I have also written to Prince Radziwill to ask him to interest himself in the affair. I beg you likewise to do what you can for me. It is a work that might likewise be useful to the Academy of Singing, for there is scarcely any portion of it that could not be almost entirely executed by voices. The more these are increased and multiplied in combination with instruments, the more effective would be the result. It ought to be appropriate also as an Oratorio, for such societies as those for the benefit of the poor require marks of this kind. Having been an invalid for some years past, and consequently my position anything but brilliant, I have had recourse to this scheme. I have written much; but as to profits, they are nearly *nil!* The more do I look upwards; but both for his own sake, and that of others, man is obliged to turn his eyes earthwards; for this, too, is part of the destiny of humanity. I embrace you, my dear fellow artist, and am, with sincere esteem,

Your friend,

BEETHOVEN.

[To Zelter.][2]

[Vienna, March 25, 1823.]

. . . I have also specially considered your proposal about your academy for singing. If the Mass is ever published, I will send you a copy free of all charge. There is no doubt that it might be almost entirely executed *à la capella:* in which case, however, the work would have to be arranged accordingly; perhaps you have patience to do this. Besides, there is already a movement in the work quite *à la capella,* and that style may be specially termed the true church style. Thanks for your wish to be of service to me, but never would I accept anything whatever from so highly esteemed an artist as yourself. I honour you, and only wish I could have an opportunity to prove this by my actions.

I am, with high consideration,

Your friend and servant,

BEETHOVEN.

---

[2]*Ibid.,* II, 110.

[To the Archduke Rudolph][3]

[Hetzendorf, July 15, 1823.]

... Will Y. R. H. be so kind as to grant me a testimonial to the following effect: "that I wrote the Grand Mass expressly for Y. R. H., that it has been for some time in your possession, and that you have been pleased to permit me to circulate it." This ought to have been the case, and being no untruth, I hope I may claim this favour. Such a testimonial will be of great service to me, for how could I have believed that my slight talents would have exposed me to so much envy, persecution, and calumny. It has always been my intention to ask Y. R. H.'s permission to circulate the Mass, but the pressure of circumstances, and above all my inexperience in worldly matters, as well as my feeble health, has caused this confusion.

If the Mass is engraved hereafter, I hope to dedicate it to Y. R. H. when published, and not till then will the limited list of royal subscribers appear. I shall ever consider Y. R. H. as my most illustrious patron, and make this known to the world whenever it is in my power. In conclusion I entreat you again not to refuse my request about the testimonial. It will only cost Y. R. H. a few lines, and ensure the best results for me. ...

To Herr Nägeli.[4]

Vienna, September 16, 1824.

My esteemed Friend,

I gladly comply with your wish that I should arrange the vocal parts of my last Grand Mass for the organ, or piano, for the use of the different choral societies. This I am willing to do, chiefly because these choral asociations by their private and still more by their church festivals make an unusually profound impression on the multitude, and my chief object in the composition of this grand Mass was to awaken, and deeply to impress, religious feelings both on singers and hearers. As, however, a copy of this kind and its repeated revision must cause a considerable outlay, I cannot, I fear, ask less than 50 ducats for it, and leave it to you to make enquiries on the subject, so that I may devote my time exclusively to it.

I am, with high consideration,
Your obedient
BEETHOVEN.

---

[3]*Ibid.,* II, 131-32.
[4]*Ibid.,* 11, 169.

Vincent Novello

(1781-1861)

In the summer of 1829, Vincent Novello undertook a tour of Europe with his wife Mary. Theirs was not simply a Continental vacation, but a sentimental journey to places that were strongholds of Mozart lore — for Novello was a passionate devotee of Mozart's music. The principal places of interest on the trip are Paris, Salzburg, and Vienna, with lesser emphasis on points between. Both Vincent and Mary left their impressions in the form of diaries, but, on the subject of church music, and especially in connection with organ playing, a skill that Vincent possessed to a high degree, it is his comments that are of most importance. His opinions are significant because he was well qualified to evaluate the religious music of the Continent as a Catholic — one of the very few who made an impression on the English musical scene — and as a well educated tourist.

Extracts from the Novello diaries

Sunday, July 5, 1829, Mannheim [1]

Went to the principal Church (formerly that of the Jesuits whose order is now suppressed) to hear High Mass which began at 9 o'clock. There was no Orchestra and the music merely consisted of a kind of Chant [*deleted:* partaking somewhat of the Chorale style] but not Gregorian: Kyrie in G, Gloria, Credo, Sanctus and Agnus in C, responses all in B flat. It was sung entirely in *unison* by Men's voices, accompanied on the Organ, as were also the Responses which were Gregorian. The soft stops were of a smooth pleasant quality, and the Full Organ, though partaking of the shrill harsh and squally kind of tone, so usual in the Continental Organs, is not deficient in grandeur and power, especially the Pedal Pipes in [the] Choir or organ *behind*. The Organists have no idea of *varying* the effect by the introduction of stops differing in

[1] *A Mozart Pilgrimage: Being the Travel Diaries of Vincent & Mary Novello in the year 1829*, Transcribed and compiled by Nerina Medici di Marignano, Edited by Rosemary Hughes (London: Novello & Co. Ltd., 1955), pp. 293-95. Reproduced by permission of the publishers, Novello & Co. Ltd., London.

the degree and quality of their tones thereby producing a gradation and contrast of effect. They use the same extremes of soft and loud throughout the service, and appear to prefer *noise* to every other effect.

The Organist on this occasion was the most steady player I have yet heard — although in the accompaniment of the Amen even he could not refrain from introducing some unnecessary nonsensical *flourishes* totally inappropriate to the Organ and quite destructive of the dignified and grave solemnity which ought to be the peculiar characteristic of the real Church style. His modulations were not distinguished by any invention — the chord of the diminished seventh too frequently used. The musical part of the service was remarkably short as it was all over in little more than half an hour.

Lutheran Church afternoon service began at 2 . . . was in time to hear a very charming old chorale steadily sung and judiciously accompanied on the organ here, which is a very good-toned one and reminded me almost of our very favourite Instrument in London, viz. the one at the Savoy Chapel. The harmonies introduced by the organist were solid and musicianlike, and it was upon the whole a respectable peformance.

I had the curiosity to stop and hear the sermon . . . the organist, who came forward and leant his head upon his hand over the railing of the Organ loft, had an intelligent countenance and bore some resemblance to the celebrated Wölfel, whom I recollect passing a very pleasant evening with at Sam Wesley's with M. Clementi. But I was sorry to find that he was a lazy fellow, for he only played a few chords, which appeared rather *in*voluntary on his part, when the People quitted the Church, instead of giving us a good fugue by Sebastian Bach as I had anticipated.

Afternoon service at the Jesuits began at 3. It is quite a different service from our Vespers. The commencement was a Hymn in the same style as the morning service, after which came a long sermon of which the congregation seemed as weary as I was, who had the advantage of not understanding it. The Preacher was a most unconscionable fellow and went on in the most persevering droning manner for near an hour. To my great relief, however, he left off at last, when the Litany of Loretto began; it was recited by one of the Priests and answered by the *Congregation* not by the Choir, and without any accompaniment whatever. After some dreary prayers, during which most of the people round me seemed inclined to indulge in a nap, came the Benediction. The Melody sung by the Choir (in *unison* still) bore some resemblance to my old favourite the 'Pange Lingua' (which to my taste is the very finest of all the Gregorian Hymns) but much inferior both in melody and modulation and dignified solemnity of expression to that exquisite specimen of sublime simplicity, and the service concluded with the same Hymn in G as that which I had before heard at the commencement and termination of the morning service. The Organist again introduced his favourite chord of the diminished seventh to absolute satiety, without seeming to be at all aware of the great variety of resolutions of which that chord is susceptible under the hands of a profound and really scientific musician.

In personal appearance he is so like my kind Ries that I could easily have taken him for a younger Brother. I noticed, in addition to what I saw in the morning, that the set of Pedals extend a 10th from G up to B. He made but little use of them, and throughout the service he introduced not a single fugal point or even a passage of imitation or piece of ingenious counterpoint. Indeed the Organists here seem to have nearly sinecure places, as far as their own extemporaneous power of invention or the elaborate performance of Fugues and other compositions of elaborate or difficult performance are concerned — any one of our own English Protestant Parish organists could have very easily got through the duty as I have heard it performed both in the morning and afternoon here.

I quite long to hear something in the style of Sebastian Bach's masterly 'Choral-Vorspiele', hitherto I have not [found] even an approach to anything at all resembling his solid and grand style of Organ Pieces.

Cathedral, Salsburg, Mass, July 16, 9 o'clock. [2]

The Service began with [a] Procession round the Church, carrying the Sacrament under a Canopy, surrounded with Priests chanting a Gregorian Hymn. A fine effect was produced by the Choristers stopping at intervals, and then breaking out again with their solemn strain, which was sung by men's voices only, and entirely unaccompanied.

The Orchestra was placed in the right-hand Gallery near the Altar against one of the large Pillars which support the Dome. It consisted of two first Violins, a second Violin, Tenor and Double Bass (no Violoncello), three Trombones (alto, tenor and bass), and the Organ. There are six Organs altogether; one against each of

[2]*Ibid.*, pp. 302-06. Reproduced by permission of the publishers, Novello & Co. Ltd., London.

the four Columns under the Dome, another small one (which is usually termed a Positif, and is something like a Chest of Drawers or sideboard) placed on the ground in the Choir not far from the High Altar, and a large Organ over the great West entrance, which Instrument was not used during any part of the service on this occasion, and seems to be reserved for the High Festivals when a more numerous Orchestra is required.

The tone of the Organ which was used to-day was of a sweet quality, especially the two Diapasons. The loud Organ, though deficient in weight and power, particularly in the low Bass Notes, is not so harsh or squally as most of the Organs which I have hitherto met with. The Organist was an unobtrusive respectable performer. He accompanied the voices judiciously, and introduced each movement of the Mass with a few Chords to decide the key. Just before the Gospel he played a little Interlude in the fugue style upon the following agreeable subject:

It was so well treated and so regular and symmetrical in design, that if it were an *extemporaneous* production, it was highly creditable to him.

There were about 6 or 8 voices, with a Person to beat the time for them, but they were not efficient, and were quite overpowered by the Instrumental Orchestra, who played too loud all the way through and especially in the *piano* parts which required delicacy. The best performers were the three trombone players, who produced a fine tone and added much grandeur to the general effect. The next best Player was on the Double Bass. He was a Priest, and it appeared to me quite a novel and singular thing to see this Instrument played by a Person in a Cassock and other sacerdotal habiliments, which however did not seem in the least to impede the freedom of his bowing.

The Responses were given by the voices alone, and were the same as those I had heard before at the Convent, viz. the mere tonic and subdominant forming the plagal cadence.

The Boys' Voices were charming and perfectly in tune; the effect of the diminuendo and gradual dying off of the sounds at the termination of each response was quite beautiful and cathedral-like. In the *Accompanied* parts of the service there was rather too much resonance and vibration from the Dome, which occasioned one Chord to run into the other so as to destroy the distinctness of the different harmonies.

The Mass was in C, but contained nothing very striking. The offertory was in E, and was the best movement that was performed. In its style it resembled the first movement of Graun's Te Deum. I endeavoured to ascertain the name of the Composer both of that, and of the rest of the Mass, but without success.

I own I was disappointed at not having heard a single Piece of Mozart's composition at any of the Churches in his own native town.

During Benediction the Performers left the Organ Gallery and stationed themselves close to the High Altar where they performed a short Motet, accompanied on the 'Positif' or small organ before mentioned.

There was no last Voluntary or 'Sortie', and the whole service was concluded in about 40 minutes.

Salzburg Cathedral, 2 o'clock afternoon.

I expected the Vespers to have begun at the above hour and accordingly attended punctually, but I found the Person at the Cathedral tuning the reed stops of the large Organ at the west end of the Church. That which they were putting into order was not a good one; the tone was *buzzy* and stifled like a poor bassoon or badly voiced Cremona.

I walked round the building and had an opportunity of examining more closely the Positif—small Organ in the Choir near the high altar. Its compass is from E in the bass 𝄢 up to C above the staff 𝄞 . It has an octave of pedals to pull down the keys but no Diapason Pipes. On the desk was an old Vellum Book in the Gregorian Character.

The Priest who had played the Double Bass in the Morning came out of the Sacristy to tune his Instrument beforehand. He seemed to be a genuine lover of the grand notes that are to be pulled out by a skilful hand from this noble Instrument. He brought out some very fine soft subdued and rich notes before he had tuned it to his mind, and as he leaned over it he appeared to doat upon its full, round and deep tones, nor did he leave it till he had put it into most admirable order.

The Choir Boys, of whom there were about a dozen, had cocked hats like the Choir Boys belonging to the King's Chapel Royal in England.

At 1/2 past 3 the Service began. There was a Catafalque under the Dome with a Mitre, Cardinal's Cap etc., and the Service seemed to be in commemoration of some elevated Ecclesiastic. The painting at the High Altar was covered with black cloth, and the Priests wore dresses similar to those I have seen in England when there has been a Requiem or Service for the dead celebrated.

After the Recitation of several Psalms by the two sides of [the] Choir taking the alternate verses — like the Decani and Cantori at our Cathedrals — there came some versicles with the following fine Responsories.

The rest of the service was solemn Gregorian and excellent of its kind, but it was not what I expected or wished to hear at the birthplace of Mozart.

Felix Mendelssohn

(1809-1847)

Remarkably few of Mendelssohn's compositions were intended for use in religious services, and of those few a large percentage was for Anglican use. The oratorios, it must be remembered, were religious in subject only, and were works for the concert hall and not the sanctuary. It is not remarkable, then, to find Mendelssohn's letters devoted almost entirely to descriptions of events, social contacts, plans for performances or new compositions, or greetings to friends and family. As a Protestant he had no reason to write a Mass, and the religious cantata was no longer a viable form in his generation. Anthems, motets, psalms, and hymns were produced in great quantity by lesser talents, and we see in Mendelssohn's output the same pattern as in that of other important composers; he devoted little time to practical music for church, and he cast his few meaningful utterances in forms that were more suitable to the public concert hall than the religious service.

[About a proposal as to some words for sacred music][1]

Düsseldorf, January 12th, 1835.

To Pastor Bauer, Belzig.

. . . What I do not understand is the purport — musical, dramatic, or oratorical, or whatever you choose to call it — that you have in view. What you mention on the subject — the time before John, and then that of John himself, till the appearance of Christ — is to my mind equally conveyed in the word "Advent," or the birth of Christ. You are aware, however, that the music must represent one particular moment, or a succession of moments; and how you intend this to be done you do not say. Actual church music, — that is, music during the Evangelical Church service, which could be introduced properly while the service was being celebrated, — seems to me impossible; and this, not merely because

---

[1] *Letters of Felix Mendelssohn Bartholdy from 1833 to 1847,* trans. by Lady Wallace (London: Longmans, Green, and Co., 1885), pp. 63-65.

I cannot at all see into which part of the public worship this music can be introduced, but because I cannot discover that *any* such part exists. Perhaps you have something to say which may enlighten me on the subject. . . . But even without any reference to the Prussian Liturgy, which at once cuts off everything of the kind, and which will, probably, neither remain as it is nor go further, I do not see how it is to be managed that music in our Church should form an integral part of public worship, and not become a mere concert, conducive more or less to piety. This was the case with Bach's "Passion;" it was sung in church as an independent piece of music, for edification. As for actual church music, or, if you like to call it so, music for public worship, I know none but the old Italian compositions for the Papal Chapel, where, however, the music is a mere accompaniment, subordinate to the sacred functions, co-operating with the wax candles and the incense, etc. If this be the style of church music that you really mean, then, as I said, I cannot discover the connecting link which would render it possible to employ it. For an oratorio, one principal subject must be adopted, or the progressive history of particular persons, otherwise the object would not be sufficiently defined; for if all is to be only contemplative with reference to the coming of Christ, then this theme has already been more grandly and beautifully treated in Handel's "Messiah," where he begins with Isaiah, and, taking the Birth as a central point, closes with the Resurrection.

When you however say "our poor Church," I must tell you what is very strange; I have found, to my astonishment, that the Catholics, who have had music in their churches for several centuries, and sing a musical Mass every Sunday if possible, in their principal churches, do not to this day possess one which can be considered even tolerably good, or in fact which is not actually distasteful and operatic. This is the case from Pergolese and Durante, who introduce the most laughable little trills into their "Gloria," down to the opera finales of the present day. Were I a Catholic, I would set to work at a Mass this very evening; and whatever it might turn out, it would at all events be the only Mass written with a constant remembrance of its sacred purpose. But for the present I don't mean to do this; perhaps at some future day, when I am older.

Thomas Hastings

(1784-1872)

The contemporaries of Lowell Mason were prolific contributors to the corpus of American hymn tunes. Hastings is said to have composed as many as a thousand, among them *Rock of Ages*. He attended a meeting of church musicians, the American Musical Convention, in 1845. A portion of the address he delivered on October 10 is given below.

Anthems[1] are of English invention, answering in some measure to the motets and cantatas of the Catholic church. The anthems of Purcel [*sic*] Croft, Green, and others of a kindred spirit, are noble specimens of composition, which have their place among the classics of the art. They should be attentively studied; though, perhaps, they will never prove to be effective instruments of edification in our American churches. They are too erudite and too diffuse; while their illustrations of the text are not sufficiently obvious to the uninitiated listener. Anthems and set pieces of a less labored character can be occasionally used with success. The number of these is increasing; and here, again, the greatest difficulty is in selection. Many are too delicate and refined for the talents of a choir or the taste of a congregation. Others are too insipid, too coarse, or too boisterous for any useful purpose. Others, still, are of too secular a character, fit only for amusement or artistical display. Those of the right character are as yet comparatively few in number. Those alone, which are found by experience to answer well the purposes of edification, can be safely employed in seasons of public worship.

And here let me observe, that unspeakable responsibilities rest upon the chorister in reference to his selections of religious music. His chants, psalms, anthems, and set pieces, should ever have a

---

[1]Source: *Proceedings of the American Musical Convention* . . . (New York: Saxton & Miles, 1845), pp. 73-74.

distinct bearing upon the other exercises of the occasion. He should fully sympathize with the officiating clergyman; and be careful to aid him in securing and preserving the right influences. By a mere disregard of this rule, the music will often become a hindrance, instead of a help, to devotion. The most fervent prayers, and the most eloquent and solemn appeals from the pulpit, will often lose their influence with the congregation through the instrumentality of some unfortunate adaptation by the chorister. Nothing is of more frequent occurrence in our worshipping assemblies; and the evil calls for the speedy application of some efficient remedy.

Raymond Seely

(dates unknown)

At the same musical meetings during which Thomas Hastings delivered the remarks on the preceding pages, the Reverend Raymond Seely addressed himself to the function of congregational singing and lamented its general absence. Since one of the recurrent questions raised at these meetings concerned the propriety and functions of the then popular "Quartet-Choirs," it is possible that his reference here is not to the larger choral groups we now hear regularly, but to the small groups of talented amateurs and skilled professionals who provided the musical treats for the Sunday services, and whose skills silenced all but the most aggressive members of the congregations.

Now,[1] we ask if the Church is not neglecting an important means for the promotion of her own prosperity when her members know little, and care less, how the music of the sanctuary is or ought to be conducted? when they are unwilling to exert themselves for its complete development as an instrument of progress, and its proper use as an ordinance of God? when they, in some instances, rest contented with, or allow of music in the house of God which would be hissed at a public concert, hooted at the evening serenade, and secretly laughed at in the parlor? We do not pretend to say when or where this is the case. But whenever and wherever it is so, instead of attracting those who have musical taste to the services of the Church, they are as directly and effectually repulsed, as though some one should stand at the door, and politely inform them that their presence within would not be agreeable; or as though a sign were placed over the entrance, bearing those ominous words, *"No admittance!"*

. . . .

---

[1]Source: *Proceedings of the American Musical Convention*, pp. 56, 62-64.

125

Our idea is this: a piece should be sung, at least once each season of divine service, in which the whole congregation should unite with the choir. For this purpose, such pieces should be selected as are well known to the congregation, and intimation, in some way, given that all are expected to take part. At other times, the music might be performed by the choir alone — the pieces being of a higher order, less known, more to their own taste, for the purpose of sustaining the interest of the singers. If, moreover, some plain and popular pieces should from time to time be selected and sung until they become familiar to the people, the number of tunes which all could sing would be increased; and the choir setting a good example, a gradual improvement in the general style of performance would take place.

But a serious objection to singing throughout the congregation is felt by the choir, lest the custom should induce scattered voices about the congregation to make attempts out of season, and thus, being out of tune, time, and place, destroy the effects of pieces which cost them much pains to bring about. This difficulty is one of importance; but it must be obviated, for the most part, by having a fair understanding with respect to the time or the piece in which all are expected to unite. If, notwithstanding, a stray voice should now and then be heard at the wrong time, the singers should comfort themselves with the reflection, that they are doing *their* duty, to the best of their ability; that they are in the house of God, not to *perform* music *for* the people, but to worship God, and to lead the people in singing his praise and making it glorious. If they were at a *concert*, the singers might complain justly of these intrusive voices; as they are in *church*, they should not permit such things to disturb them.

But admitting the validity of these objections against congregational singing, still greater evils arise from confining this department of divine worship to the choir.

It fosters the harmful notion that the object of the choir is to *perform* music *for* the church, rather than to unite *with* the church while leading in its devotions. That this is the effect appears in the objection to stray voices in the congregation, just mentioned. It leads to an ambition for display among the members of the choir, all wishing to gain credit by the performance, and some desiring to attract notice to themselves. Moreover, while confining the music to the choir leads the singers to regard themselves as mere performers, it also has a tendency to produce the impression on their minds *that they are not in church at all.* The introduction of curtains about the choir has so increased this tendency that, in many cases, the singers seem to regard themselves as a company entirely distinct from the rest of the people, like fiddlers perched up in their box in a cotillion room, rather than members of a worshipping assembly.

Another evil resulting from the custom of regarding the choir as performers for, rather than leaders in the worship of the people, is felt more especially in the country churches; where the congregation becomes so entirely dependent on the choir, that it rests with a few leading singers to decide whether the church shall have any music at all in its services. In this way some churches have, at times, been forced to omit this part of public worship altogether.

But where matters do not proceed to this extreme, it is generally or often the case, that the members of the choir are expected to *perform* music at the meetings for social prayer also. This, in itself considered, is both incongruous and wrong. It is incongruous; for, in the very idea of these meetings, the union of all in the work of praise is included; it is wrong; for when the singers neglect to attend, this part of worship must be dispensed with.

Samuel Sebastian Wesley

(1810-1876)

The generation of Wesleys following that of the brothers who established Methodism was associated strongly with music, even though the new religious practice held little of promise to one who would make his career in church music. Charles (1757-1834) was a capable performer who mastered the craft of composition, but fell short of developing it to a true artistic level. Samuel (1766-1837), considerably more talented, became a Roman Catholic before age twenty, and was an advocate of the music of J. S. Bach. An unfortunate accident limited his musical activities both as a performer and composer. His son, Samuel Sebastian, was associated with the Church of England—having been trained in the Chapel Royal—and established a fine reputation as an organist, being known also as a competent composer. His pamphlet on cathedral music reflects the lack of financial support and thoughtful concern that was endangering the elaborate ritual music of his day. The other documents appearing in this century prove that the problem lay not only in England's cathedrals and large parish churches, but in the unsettled relationship between the Church and music on almost every front.

In recent attempts to form Choirs[1] and establish the Musical Service of the Church, discretion, in the choice of Compositions for public use, has been altogether wanting. Under a false belief that homage was being paid to the Church School, Composition, shorn of every effective quality, has been advanced, on the score of its age and its appearance in long notes, (minims and semibreves.) An essential feature this! Some would reject all Music but the unisonous Chants of a period of absolute barbarism,—which they term "Gregorian." All is "Gregorian" that is in the black, diamond, note! These men would look a Michael Angelo in the face and tell him Stonehenge was the perfection of architecture!

---

[1]Source: Samuel Sebastian Wesley, *A few Words on Cathedral Music and the Musical System of the Church, with a Plan of Reform* (London: F. & J. Rivington, 1849), pp. 49-62. Reprinted, London: Hinrichsen Edition, 1961.

They think they are conforming to the Church-musical system by forming "a Choir," (such a Choir as had better not be described, perhaps,) and appointing a "Precentor," (neither shall the Precentor be described:) but they are not so doing. The Church system admits, nay compels, our enriching the Service with every excellence the progress of time affords, in conformity with her school; and these amateur efforts claim severer reprobation than is here ventured on, for their effect can only be that of suggesting to the higher powers in the Church how worthless a thing Church music is, and how unnecessary or wrong it is to attach any importance whatever to it at the present day.

In restoring the Musical Service of the Church should we consult the antiquary or the connoisseur? It is not by a mere repetition of what took place formerly that we can effectually "restore." The improved state of public taste must be remembered, and the giant strides of Secular Art. The Sacred must be made to stand in the same position with regard to the Secular as formerly, and to effect this is assuredly no easy task. Public approbation should not be sought in the shape of mere dutiful respect or antiquarian prejudice; congregations should not be required to adopt indifferent specimens on the score of duty, or of age. The present state of the art, and of public taste, is such as to warrant our claiming for Church Music the sympathetic regard arising from involuntary but well grounded admiration. Without deferring too much to public opinion, we may hope that its criticism will be searching in all cases where the Choral Service of the Church is in process of restoration. The art is in more danger from those who, upon the score of a little knowledge, dispense with professional advice, than from others who, having no technical acquaintance with the subject, adjust by the feelings of the heart alone the standard of their taste.

This exalting the past upon the ruin of the present is unjustifiable. This country will never again be without talent which can impart to Church Music the highest qualities of art; and, in connection with the Service, give beauty where beauty is required, grandeur where it is effective, and solemnity where the subject demands it: which can, by a proper train of musical thought and expression, denote praise, supplication, or thanksgiving, in a manner far above the reach of those who saw but "as through a glass darkly;" who were but pioneers in a science which may be destined to go on from strength to strength, until we "again renew that song," that "fair music," which, in the words of Milton, "disproportioned sin" is said to have "broke;"

when we may all, musically as well as morally, find the consummation of all things to be the period at which alone perfection is attained.

How different a picture is presented in the sister arts! The highest order of talent in them is appreciated, and a source of fortune and honour secured to its possessor. The work of a few days produces for the artist a sum of money greater than the work of a life (of the lives of many) would to the Church musician. Mr. Landseer, it is said, has in eight days painted the picture of a horse for which he has received a thousand guineas.

Turn we to Cathedrals. Were the musician who should produce a work of the highest merit in eight days, to ask, not a thousand guineas, but a thousand shillings, pence, farthings, the reply would be, invariably, "NO!" Let him study hard in his art, from the age of eight to thirty-five, sacrificing every interest to this one sole pursuit, let him offer his work as a present to *some* Cathedrals, and *they would not go to the expense of copying out the parts for the Choir!*

It is here, asserted as a fact, that the late Mr. Attwood, organist of St. Paul's Cathedral and composer to Her Majesty's Chapels, a pupil of Mozart, when he wished the performance of any new composition at the Royal Chapel, was compelled to furnish the copies requisite for the Choir at this own expense; for, the Authorities would not pay for the copying!

When Dr. Boyce published his *Cathedral Music*, so inadequate was the reward which he met with from the Chapters, that a very heavy loss to him was the result; and this notwithstanding the fact of the Music of the Church having been so injured or destroyed during the Civil War that scarcely anything remained for Cathedral use.

The late Samuel Wesley published a most beautiful and masterly "Service" for Cathedrals. Only one Cathedral purchased copies, and the plates were eventually melted down by the publisher, Balls, of Oxford Street, to be re-stamped with a set of Quadrilles.

There are references to the mere purchasing of printed copies of great works by Cathedrals. It is here seen that even when such works are to be had at the mere cost of paper and printing, a deaf ear is turned. Little chance is there of *copyright* being held in respect. If a composer wishes to obtain the suscription of Cathedrals to a work designed for their exclusive use, he may obtain some little support here and there, but some of the replies sent by Chapters on such occasions would surprise the reader by their want of every thing like appreciation of either the artist, his art, or the undeniable claims of the Choral Service.

On a recent application of the kind being made to the Organist of a Cathedral — not the Chapter — he replied: "I am glad you do not ask me to get our Chapter to subscribe to your work. They never spend a pound to purchase music; and if they did, the Choir is in such a wretched state, we could not sing it."

Instances without end occur to the writer, but he forbears. Let those who are either disposed to question, or interested to deny, his assertions, point out, if they can, *one single instance* of liberal and judicious encouragement having, within living memory, been extended to the higher departments of musical science at Cathedrals.[a]

It should here, however, be in fairness stated, that the claims of this subject seem to have far outgrown the amount of aid which might reasonably be expected to proceed exclusively from Capitular bodies. Music has progressed with giant strides since the period at which Cathedrals were endowed. Music is now the study of a life, and its professors are, it is believed, far more numerous than the Clergy themselves. The claims of music in public estimation are seen in its universal adoption as a branch of education in the middle and upper circles; in its influence in the cause of charity at festival performances; in the vast and increasing attention it receives from tens of thousands of the people; and above all, in its close connection with even the most imperfect celebrations of Divine worship, and where even the smallest funds in its behalf are only obtained with great difficulty. From these circumstances, music, to receive any justice in its religious uses, must now become a more expensive item in Church outlay than hitherto, and in pointing, as is the object of these pages, to merely a minimum state, it were hopeless and unfair to ask Capitular bodies to supply of themselves the necessary funds for even this.[b] But, an appeal to the public, under their sanction, would undoubtedly receive a warm and liberal response; and why has this not been made? As has been herein stated, the claims of the subject have been, in some degree, from time to time submitted to our Clergy; but a minute professional statement, having reference to all necessary details, has, it is allowed, *never* been entered into.

---

[a] Here and there a singer or two have been added to the Choir, and an organ improved.

[b] Chapter property would seem to be by no means great when all necessary outgoings are considered. Of the importance of a "learned leisure" for the Clergy there cannot be a question. What father will permit his child to enter the profession, if poverty be entailed? And should pulpits be consigned to the illiterate and unworthy? The incomes of Church Dignitaries must appear small in the sight of manufacturers and persons engaged in trade of even inferior standing.

The musical profession can hardly be blamed for this. It is repulsive to them to obtrude the claims of their art on the Church, and to speak of religion and money, as they needs must, in one and the same breath. They feel, also, that the Clergy either systematically disparage music, or at best view it with a cold side glance, and have ever done so since the reign of Elizabeth; and this for no better reason than that the interests of religion were far above those of music; and that the claims of a vastly increasing population have been great and pressing. On this ground have they in later years permitted the spoliation of Choirs; and from this cause, even at the present day, is it most difficult to awaken the authorities to the interests of music. It was the same with respect to the higher branches of architecture until a very recent date. Would that the claims of music could be as easily explained and understood as those of the comparatively simpler principles of architecture.

The subject having thus been generally considered, with respect to, first, the number of persons essential to the formation of a Choir, secondly, the necessity of a Musical Head or Principal to that Choir; and thirdly, the School of Music employed by the Church in her Services, and the propriety of carrying forward and enlarging its boundaries; let us now refer briefly to the working details by which these objects may be effected.

THE PLAN

which the writer would suggest for remedying the evils of which he so deplores the existence, is as follows: —

The number of lay Choir-men in daily attendance should never be less than *twelve,* this being the *least* number by which the choral service can be properly performed.

To ensure the constant attendance of *twelve* it would be necessary to retain at least three *additional* voices (one of each kind) to meet the frequent deficiencies arising from illness or other unavoidable causes. The stipend of the former might be £85 per annum; of the latter £52.

These lay singers should be required to give the degree of attention to *rehearsals* and every other musical duty exacted of all such persons at ordinary performances of music, and, like others, they should be subject to an early removal in cases of wilful inattention.

Should it not be deemed desirable for them to occupy themselves in trade, or other pursuits, (and that it is *not* desirable cannot be a question, their Cathedral duty, if properly followed, being the work of a life,) the salaries should be higher, and not less than from £100 to £150 per annum.[c]

The election to the office of lay Choir men should rest with the organists or musical conductors of three Cathedrals, namely the one in which the vacancy occurs, and the two nearest to it, the Dean and Chapter of the former exercising their judgment as to the religious fitness of the candidate. In fixing, as is here proposed, the number of the lay singers at the *minimum* number, twelve, it may be added, that in any Cathedral town where the musical services of the Cathedral were conducted in a meritorious manner, they would undoubtedly enjoy great popularity, and enlist the voluntary aid of many competent persons. An addition of *six* such might probably be relied on; and this, although inadequate — the requirements of such large buildings as our Cathedrals being considered — would be a great advance upon present things.[d]

A Musical College, in connection with one of the Cathedrals, and under the government of its Dean and Chapter, seems indispensably necessary for the tuition of lay singers; and, what is more important, for the complete education of the higher order of musical officer employed as the Organist, Composer, or Director of the Choir. Lay singers for Cathedrals are not easily procured; and the above arrangement would greatly facilitate the object of providing every Cathedral with the required number for its Choir, and for imparting a thorough and complete musical education to the musical professors employed by the Church. A School of this kind might not be self-supporting, possibly; every Cathedral, therefore, should be required to contribute something to its maintenance.

The Cathedral Organist should, in every instance, be a professor of the highest ability, — a master in the most elevated departments of composition, — and efficient in the conducting and super-intendance of a Choral body.

The Art of Music is indeed a different affair to what it was four centuries ago. It might not be very rash to assert that it has now reached perfection, humanly speaking. Nothing can exceed the fugues ·of Bach, the melody of Mozart, or the orchestral

---

c The constant vibration of the lay clerk between his shop and his Cathedral, as at present, is productive of serious results; rendering him, but too often, a tradesman amongst singers, and a singer amongst tradesmen. The serving two masters is disastrous, as inquiry into the position of these parties at the present time would show.

d At Leeds Parish Church, where the Choral Service is performed, and supported by voluntary contributions, several gentlemen attend on this footing, and with regularity and good effect.

arrangement of Spohr. The Science is now the study of one man's life: and how few attain excellence!

To provide each Cathedral with a Professor who should be excellent in every department of his Art,[e] and who had made the Church School the foundation of *all*, is a desideratum. In aid of this *the College* would do much. Elections need not, however, be made exclusively from thence. Great talent should ever find its market; but in all vacancies the elective body might be the seven Professors of the seven Cathedrals nearest the vacancy. In this, as in the case of the lay singers, there should be given to the Clergy a veto in respect to the moral and religious fitness of the candidate, and no more. This would assuredly be an unexceptionable mode of election; and, indeed, it were useless to endow offices, were not the most unexceptionable means, in all cases, adopted for filling them.[f]

With regard to the emoluments of this officer, but a few words shall suffice. At the present time the Organist's salary is about £200 a year; but in populous and wealthy districts this forms but a small item in his actual income. If he be a clever pianist and teacher of singing, an industrious use of these acquirements will produce him from one to two thousand a year. The London professor, if *eminent*, obtains far more than this. He makes a fortune in not many years. And there are many mere teachers in London, men of simple industry, who "work like moles," whose "names are never heard," but who "teach" from six in the morning to ten at night throughout a life, and acquire great fortunes.

There should not be awarded to the Cathedral Professor the full amount these teachers earn, or what he himself could earn by devoting himself to the secular branches of his art. The privilege of devoting himself exclusively to his Cathedral duty and self-improvement, would of itself be an immense inducement· to men of that high order from which alone he should be chosen. He should be prohibited from ever giving a single lesson of the popular kind in question, and be compelled to devote himself exclusively to the high objects of his calling; and to enable him to do this, he should have awarded to him just enough to dispel

---

e A man must know all Schools to write unexceptionably in any.

f At the present time, a very common practice at Cathedrals is to elect the *Deputy* Organist on a vacancy when it occurs; and a small amount of musical talent is accepted in such cases, upon the score of "general good conduct," "unexceptionable character," "long connection with the Cathedral," and so forth. By this means is talent rebuked; and when it is seen that men of high attainments never can condescend to the office of *Deputy* Organists, our Chapters surely should prove themselves above local influences on such occasions.

anxiety in pecuniary affairs. If salaries of from £500 to £800 a year be suggested for the Provincial Organists, or Musical Directors of Cathedrals, it will be said how many Curates there in the Church at a salary of £60 or £80 per annum? But it is not here a question of men standing at the threshold of their profession. The artists pointed to are the *bishops* of their calling — men consecrated by their genius, and set apart for duties which only the best talent of the kind can adequately fulfil. [9]

Efforts in Musical Composition for the Church claim no public encouragement, and are not intended to excite admiration and applause. They are designed to promote the solemnity of Divine worship, and give a larger emphasis to passages of Holy Scripture. The highest talent is required; the utmost genius may be absorbed in the work; and yet it is beyond the power of the people to promote such efforts further than by insisting that, as heretofore, the necessary support shall be provided within the Church by means of an endowed musical appointment at each Cathedral, some enlargement of the Organist's office which shall compensate him for the devotion of his whole time to the work.

---

[9] The salary of the two London appointments, St. Paul's, and Westminster Abbey, might be higher.

It may be that eminent musicians might object to cancel their valuable engagements and to forego the pleasure of comparative independence, for a life of incessant duty at a country Cathedral, and that what has been herein stated may militate against the fairness of these proposals, when, as for instance, the fact of an artist obtaining for his picture, — the work of a few days, — a higher price than that proposed to be attached to a whole year's professional service at a Cathedral.

But however popular music may become, it is a question whether the composer will ever obtain the same rate remuneration as the painter and the sculptor, by mere efforts in composition. In painting, too, as in music, an inferior branch is the most profitable: portrait painting, in the one; piano-forte tuition, in the other. A man with a genius for the higher branches of musical composition, will generally, no doubt, cancel every other occupation for the loved one of devoting himself to that end; and a comparatively small income, which offers the desired facilities, be preferred to any other means of livelihood.

Lowell Mason

(1792-1872)

His name is known to every student of music education, his hymn tunes are familiar to most Protestant denominations, and his reputation as a compiler and arranger of European works for American singers is widely recognized. Still, Lowell Mason's original anthems, some of them excellent for their time, are hardly known, and his volume of letters, written to report the activities of his European tour of 1852-53, is still mistakenly attributed to his earlier trip by *Grove's Dictionary* and other sources. The letters, products of his mature years, are careful evaluations and comparisons of musical practices by an experienced and practical man. To read his description of the Thomaskirche and its Order of Service a century after Bach's death is interesting; to examine the description printed here of the Berlin Dom-Chor is to feel his great interest and enthusiasm for fine religious music. Not only does he describe the musical qualities of that group, but he provides us, by his comparisons, with a clear picture of the quality and practice of the best American groups of that same time.

The Dom-Kirche, or Cathedral — The Exercises[1]

Berlin, April, 1852

There is no choir of music in Berlin, and perhaps none in the world equal to that of the Dom-Kirche, or Cathedral. This choir is very celebrated; it is the same choir, a part of which gave concerts in London in the summer of 1851. It is said to be even better than the far-famed choir at Rome. We attended three distinct services at the cathedral, and heard the choir each time. It consists of about fifty singers; the treble and the alto parts are sung by boys. It is arranged in double chorus, and the music of the old composers, in eight parts, is often performed; so that one may hear Palestrina, Lotti, Durante and others of the Italian school; Bach, Graun and others of the German school, together with the best

[1]Source, Lowell Mason, *Musical Letters from Abroad* (New York: Mason Brothers, 1854; reprint, New York: Da Capo Press, 1967), pp. 105-08, 111-15.

modern authors. We infer from their collections of music, however, that they confine themselves almost exclusively to the *ecclesiastical style*, for we find their books contain nothing in the manner of Haydn's or Mozart's hymns, motets, or masses, or like other modern orchestral vocal music. The choir is entirely professional—that is, the singers are such by profession; they have learned to sing, and that is their business or calling. The boys who sing the upper parts are trained daily, and are preparing in their turn to be professors, teachers and composers of music, vocalists or instrumentalists, here or elsewhere. The parts are, of course, well balanced as to power, and the chorus of men's voices (tenors and basses) singing in unison, as they often do, is peculiarly grand and effective. In addition to the regular choir, there is a preparatory department, consisting of some twenty or thirty fine-looking little boys, of from eight to ten years of age. These are candidates for future membership, and form a juvenile choir; they stand on one side of the choir, and lead in the congregational singing, thus affording relief to the regular choir, and giving them time to breathe and recruit. We have said that these boys *stand:* this is equally true of others, for there are no seats in the organ-loft, and the members of the choir all stand during the whole service. The various exercises are distributed between the choir, the people, and the minister, so as to hold the attention and keep all employed. Those parts of the service which are performed by the choir, or by the people, are *sung,* and the part belonging to the minister is *read.* In this respect, the service is unlike that of the Lutheran churches in Saxony, where the minister's part is chanted, or uttered in singing tones. The *musical* forms of the choir performance are motets, (anthems they would be called, perhaps, with us,) short responsive sentences, in harmony parts, or unison, or a plain syllabic chant, with Hallelujahs, Hosannas and Amens. The *poetic* forms are mostly from Scripture, though sometimes metrical hymns are sung by the choir, but these are usually sung by the congregation. The *musical* form of the congregation is, of course, that of the *chorale,* and is Old Hundredth, St. Ann's, or York-like. The congregational tunes are sung much slower than we heard them in England, and about the time similar tunes have been generally sung in America. There is not an instant during the service that is unoccupied, one exercise following another without the least pause, so that the minister's voice seems to be joined on to the choir performance, or to the organ, or *vice versâ*. There is no interruption of the devotional exercises, by rubrical directions—"Let us sing," "Please to sing," "Omitting such and such stanzas," or by reading over a hymn before it is sung, as with us; the hymns to be sung are known the moment one enters the church, their numbers being suspended on tablets in various parts of the house, so that they may be seen by all; and the particular hymn that is about to be sung, or that is being sung, is known by the tablet in front of the organ-loft, which contains the number of that only, so that any one coming in after the service has been commenced, has only to turn his eyes towards the choir-tablet, and he knows immediately where to find his place. The organ is not played when the choir sing, but is used only for voluntaries, intermediate responses, interludes or transludes, and for accompanying the congregation when all unite in the song. There are no interludes either between the lines of a stanza, as in Saxony, or between the stanzas, as with us. The fashion of organ-interludes in hymn-tunes, seems to be passing away; and I observed, when in England, that they were but seldom introduced there.

The service is entirely liturgic, or is pre-composed, no provision being made, that I could perceive, for extemporary performances. Yet the same liturgy is not always used, but there are different liturgies for different occasions. The most interesting service I attended was one for Passion Week, and which was used twice during the week. There was no sermon, or anything in homiletic form, but only devotional exercises, in connection with Scriptural readings. The time occupied was an hour and twenty minutes; and of this I should judge that an hour at least was occupied by the singing exercises of the choir, or congregation, and only about twenty minutes by the readings (prayers and lessons) of the minister; yet the minister stood during the whole service in front of the altar; and the whole congregation stood also during most of the service, the king himself, who was present, setting the example. The organ-loft is in a gallery immediately back of the altar; so that the congregation, when they face the minister, face the choir also. . . .

. . . .

But to the choir again. It is hardly necessary to say, that its members seem to be perfect with respect to all the technicals of singing, such as the formation of the voice, utterance of words, and of tone, time, tune, pitch, &c. To all these things they have been *trained;* they have formed correct habits with regard to them, so that singing out of time or tune, falling from the pitch, bad tone, or inarticulate delivery of words or of tones, are never expected, thought of, or heard, and certainly would not be tolerated for a moment. They have a regular conductor, who stands in view of all the members, directs the time, and indicates such other things as are usual with the baton. But it is not only with these preliminary pre-requisites that the members of this choir are familiar; they seem to know what belongs to the higher departments of taste and expression, and in their performances they make such a practical application of the dynamic degrees and tones, as to bring out in a much more satisfactory manner than is often heard, the signs of a deep internal feeling; and all the externals seem to say that the spirit of worship may be there. We do not mean to say that all the people, or all the members of the choir, or the minister, *are* or *are not* true spiritual worshipers; this we do not know, but we think that such a *form* is presented, both as respects the matter and the manner in song and in speech, as is well adapted to the spirit of worship, and to aid the true worshiper in his sincere attempts to worship "in spirit and in truth."

We do not suppose it to be possible to train a choir of boys of twelve or fourteen years of age, to sing independently with any high degree of expression, (except so far as it may be done by imitation,) not even if the true spirit and worship is in the heart; the immaturity of taste and judgment belonging to their age must prevent this; but yet, something may be done, as is proved by the boys of the Dom-Chor; and certainly a much higher degree of excellence may be attained anywhere by *trained boy's voices.* than by *untrained female voices.* or such female voices as may sometimes be heard in our choirs. I presume there is no choir to be found in which a higher degree of excellence exists than in that of the Dom-Kirche; it is certainly much in advance of such of the English cathedral choirs as we have heard. That union or blending of the voices by which true chorus effect is produced, and without which it cannot exist, is realized in a high degree. Some exception must however be made here, with respect to the union of *boys'* with *men's* voices; but this blending of the voices of the *Dom-Chor* is admirable, and when the tenors and basses are singing by themselves, or even when the altos unite, it is almost perfect; but the soprano of the boys, especially if it be above the twice marked small *c.* is so different in quality or character, that *that* close union by which many voices become *one.* is not attainable. In the English choirs there is indeed none of this blending, and the soprano of the boys stands out quite disconnected from the other parts. The choirs are so small, too, that this of itself is sufficient to prevent the effect of which we speak; for it is a well-known fact, that it cannot be easily attained with a less number of voices than about six on a part; but it seems not to be sought after in these choirs, so that in respect to this point, a choral performance in one of the English cathedrals, reminds one of Nebuchadnezzar's image, partly of brass and partly of clay. Not so, however, in the great musical festival choirs of England, or in those societies where a female soprano is employed, for in both these we have heard such a perfect union of fully-developed male and female voices, as to leave nothing more on this point to be desired.

The points which struck us the most forcibly with respect to the *external* of the singing of this choir, are *first*, the *decision* and *firmness* with which the tones are taken or delivered, and this is equally applicable to piano and to forte passages; and *second*, the *perfect truthfulness with which the pitch is held* by the mere voices alone, for the organ, as we have already remarked, is not played when the choir sing, but is only brought in to aid the congregational chorus; then indeed its pipes are not spared; but the greater part of the musical exercises are by the choir, *senza stromenti*. The choir seem no more to need the accompaniment of an organ, than does a well-organized and perfect orchestra; and the use of the vocal organs of the one seems to be as *firm, decided, and true to the pitch,* as are the *bows, strings,* and *mouth-pieces* of the other. A *third* point in which this choir excels — the *great* point — has already been spoken of, but yet we wish to add a few words on the *appropriate expression* which marks their singing. It is *tasteful,* or it conforms to the generally-received laws of taste in choir and orchestral performances. It is easy and natural, without any approach to coarseness, roughness, or crudeness, on the one hand, or affectation of beauty, or elegance, or feeling on the other. There is an absence of that stiffness or formality too often witnessed, and especially of that mechanical straining for effect which is apt to characterize the performance of such choirs as depend upon a marked hymn book, and endeavor to obtain expression from noted directions. True expression can only proceed from a well-educated taste, an instantaneous appreciation of beauty, a quick sensibility, and a warm and sympathizing heart; and this is equally true, both in elocution and in song.

That the choir of the Dom-Kirche is the best in the world, (as we have heard it called,) we do not know, but that it is, on the whole, the best we have heard, we are willing to admit; and the performances of the choir and congregation, separately and together present us with as fine a form of church music as we may ever expect to witness in this world.

We cannot close these very imperfect remarks on the music of
the Dom-Kirche, without contrasting for a moment, the form of
church music which it presents, with one which prevails to a
considerable degree with us. What would the quartet clubs of our
churches do, if they should become familiar with such choir
singing as we have attempted to describe? If governed by correct
musical taste, or by religious propriety, and if uninfluenced by
that, the love of which is the root of all evil, we think they would,
at least, draw the curtains in front of the organ-loft closer than
ever, or perhaps hang their four-stringed harps on the willows, and
let the people sing their own songs, until a choir, properly so
called, could be formed. What worshipping assembly, *knowing* the
power of a good choir, would be satisfied for a single Sabbath
with the drawing-room effects of a single voice on a part? The
substitution of a piano forte for an organ in church worship,
would not be in worse taste than the substitution of a quartet for
a choir. A quartet is beautiful in its place, and in connection and
in contrast with a choir, may be truly effective in church music,
but save us from that form of song in the house of God, which
consists in the monotony of a four-voiced performance, without
the light and shade afforded by a chorus.   Again, the true form
of church music can only be found in the union of a choir,
(including solo and quartet,) with a congregational performance.
And while these two combined present us with a most perfect
form of church song, each must be kept in its own proper place;
they must be related and dependent, and yet preserve their own
independence. Choir singing must be one thing, and
congregational singing another, both with respect to the character
of the music and the style of the performance. Congregational
singing can never be good, until such tunes as are now attempted
are laid aside, and a plainer and easier class are alone encouraged.
No German congregation could sing such tunes as St. Martin's,
Abridge, Devizes, and a host of others, old and new, now supposed
to be appropriate to congregational performance in America; but
let a plain and simple style of tunes be sung, such as are sung
here, and let the more difficult and more tasteful pieces be
reserved for a well-trained choir, and then both may flourish,
strengthening in each other's strength. It is a grand mistake, but
one that has extensively prevailed, to suppose that these two forms
of church music are antagonistic, so that if one is encouraged, the
other must be discouraged. They are friendly, and should ever go
hand in hand.

Once more—the account given of the Dome Choir should not

discourage such choirs in our country, as can never expect to equal, or indeed to come near to that, in the excellency of their performances. *That* is a professional choir, sustained at a great expense, and of course, the circumstances under which it prospers are quite unlike anything existing in our country. *Ours* must be voluntary choirs of amateurs, supporting themselves, and in most cases paying their own expenses. But yet, if those who have good voices will but apply themselves according to their opportunity, as much may be done by our choirs, to promote the cause of a spiritual and sincere worship in America, as is done by the more skilful, better trained, and better paid choirs in Germany.

Cardinal Patri

(November 18-20, 1856)

The General Directions o November, 1856, reflect some of the ideas that were propagandized by the leaders of the Cecilian Movement. The period between this document and the one a century earlier had seen produced the Masses of Haydn, Schubert, Berlioz, Bellini, and many others who represented the reformers. It is, however, significant to recognize that what was tolerated in the nineteenth century had been forbidden in the eighteenth. Despite the attempts to restore plainsong and Renaissance polyphony, the Church was accepting solos and ensembles so long as they avoided theatrical style, orchestras so long as they were not too noisy or predominant over the voices, and substitutes for plainsong Introits and Antiphons so long as they were sung "in a respectful manner." It may be that we should construe the increasing number and length of pronouncements as evidence of the greater encroachment of secular style into the Church despite the best efforts of the Cecilians.

General Directions of November 18, 1856,
and Instructions for Directors of Music of
November 20, 1856, Cardinal Patri, Vicar of Rome[1]

Resumé

1. Church music should differ from profane and theatrical music, not only *melodically*, but also in its *form, substance* and *atmosphere*. Consequently, the following are forbidden:

   a) *Themes* which suggest the theatre and which are not directly inspired by the words.

   b) *Rapid and restless movements:* for, when the words express joy and exultation, these sentiments must not be given a musical setting which suggests the gaiety of the dance, but one which brings out the calm joy of religion.

2. The words must always be pronounced clearly and with the

---

[1] *Papal Documents on Sacred Music,* p. 6. Reprinted by permission of *Sacred Music,* Journal of The Church Music Association of America.

143

rapidity of ordinary speech.

3. The words must be set to music in such a way as to retain their proper order; and while it is allowable, after having sung a full and intelligible idea, to repeat certain words or phrases, this must be done without inverting the order of the words, or confusing the meaning; moreover, it must be done with moderation; nor is it permitted to add to the text other words which are foreign to it, or to omit any of those which are contained therein.

4. It is forbidden to sing *arias*, duets, trios, etc., having the same character and structure as those of the theatre.

5. Instrumental music is forbidden unless with special permission. The use of drums, *timpani* (kettledrums), cymbals, all instruments of percussion and those which are noisy, is forbidden.

6. In compositions for the Church, long introductions or preludes are forbidden, whether these be for full orchestra or for individual instruments.

7. Composers of Church music must always bear in mind that instrumental music in church is merely *tolerated:* it must serve primarily to sustain and enrich the chant, never to dominate it, still less to overpower it and reduce it to a mere accessory.

8. Organists are forbidden to perform pieces taken, in whole or in part, from the theatre; also to play brilliant pieces which are distracting, for, on the contrary, music must be made a means of recollection and must serve to excite the devotion of the faithful.

9. It is forbidden to develop certain psalms with great elaboration and with full orchestra, while passing over the other psalms and the hymn with indecent haste and with organ accompaniment. Each part of the Mass and of Vespers must be set to music and rendered in the same manner.

10. Each chant of Mass and of Vespers must preserve its *unity as a composition*, consequently it is forbidden to separate unduly with musical interludes, one part of a chant from another.

11. Those who are incapable of singing the Introit of the Mass and the Antiphons of Vespers in Gregorian Chant, may sing them to other melodies, but always in a respectful manner and so that at least the sacred words may be pronounced distinctly and with religious gravity.

12. Choirmasters and organists who fail to observe these rules will be fined *five scudi* ($5.00), which fine will be doubled or even tripled should the offence be repeated; but, after a third offence, they will henceforth be forbidden to direct music or play the organ in Church.

13. Rectors of Churches will be fined *ten scudi* ($10.00) for infraction of these rules, which fine may be doubled or trebled and to which other punishments may be added.

14. A *Commission of Vigilance* is hereby formed, a certain number of whose members must be drawn from the Congregation of St. Cecilia.

Frederick Arthur Gore Ouseley

(1825-1889)

One of the last staunch defenders of the English cathedral tradition, Ouseley composed a corpus of traditionally correct, but dull, anthems in the same decades when his more succesful competitors were Goss, Tours, and Stainer. Apparently he was aware that the world he reflected in his music was not to continue unchanged, for his concluding words to his edition of Naumann's popular history book show his understanding of the importance of the new systems of learning to read music — systems that eventually brought English music to appear in Tonic Sol-Fa editions for the use of amateur singers.

We must [1] . . . say a few words about the astonishing improvement which has taken place in the Church music of England during the last half-century. This is mostly due to the formation of choral unions and associations in connection with the different dioceses or archdeaconries, and may be considered to have been indirectly a consequence of the spread of the well-known system of teaching music to large classes which was introduced by Dr. John Hullah. [2] These choral unions employ teachers who go about among the various parish choirs, training them upon a uniform system, and thus preparing them for collective meetings at various central churches, where great effects are produced by the large bodies of rural choristers who join the service. In some cathedrals over two thousand voices have sometimes been thus brought together with the happiest results. The whole country has been now brought under this excellent organization, more or less, and a vastly increased interest in Church music has been the

---

[1]Emil Naumann, *The History of Music,* trans. F. Praeger, ed. Rev. Sir F. A. Gore Ouseley (2 vols.; London: Cassell & Company, [1886]), II, 1313-14.

[2]John Pyke Hullah (1812-1884), singer and church organist. During some of his visits to Paris, he became interested in the system of mutual instruction in music that was developed by Guillaume-Louis Wilhem [recte Bocquillon] (1781-1842). He adapted the system to English use, opened the Singing School of Schoolmasters in 1841, and became the center of much controversy, in the course of which thousands of people came under the influence of his system.

natural result. Choral services may now be heard in many a village church, where formerly only a few bad voices roared or howled to the accompaniment of a barrel-organ, or to that of a few rural fiddlers in a gallery. It is impossible to overrate the importance of this onward step from every point of view, and it is a pleasant feature to contemplate in the general aspect of musical culture and development in England.

R. B. Daniel

(dates unknown)

One of the vexing questions in performance practice concerns the time and place that first finds women singing in choirs with men at regularly constituted church services. Obviously the practice changes with various countries and dogmas, and our evidence is spread thinly among references by Burney, the early American writers, the papal documents, and various brief, but often strongly worded references. To those other generally known sources, we may add the opinions of the Reverend R. B. Daniel, of whom we know only that he was sometime organist of the parish churches of St. Mary Bredin and St. Mary Bredman, Canterbury, and Curate of Tickenhall, Derby. His words appear nearly half a century after Lowell Mason's less extensive ideas on this subject. It appears possible that he was late in expressing himself because he felt the necessity to speak against some of the changes that the Oxford Movement had brought to Anglican practice.

Women and Boys in Church Choirs [1]

Among the many and various changes affecting Church music that have been made during the last quarter of a century, the substitution of boys' voices in choirs for those of women is not one of the least important. Once hardly to be seen anywhere in church choirs, boys now are found in very many places; not only in large towns, but also in small towns and villages, they are often to be seen occupying the choirseats formerly occupied by women. The fancy that the *soprano* parts in our Church music ought to be rendered by boys, and not by women, has spread throughout the length and breadth of the land, seizing on place after place like an epidemic.

The causes that have favoured its spread are: certain objections which it has become fashionable to make to the employment of women in choirs, and the desire for surpliced choirs, of which

---

[1] R. B. Daniel, *Chapters on Church Music* (London: Elliot Stock, 1894), pp. 145-49, 155-56.

women cannot be members. Sometimes boys have been introduced into choirs at the suggestion of influential members of the congregation, who have heard the service at some cathedral, and, pleased with the singing of the boys, have thought that they ought to have boy singers at their own churches at home, forgetting that the singing of *their* boys will be very different from that of the cathedral boys whose performance pleased them so much. People also have assisted to spread the fancy by claiming for boys that they sing better than women.

Those who consider the singing of boys, speaking generally, to be greatly inferior to that of women, and believe that it cannot, by any training, be rendered more than tolerable, and yet think that women ought not to sing in choirs, maintain that women do not look well in the chancel, and that the tone-quality of the female voice renders it unsuitable for use in the church. They object that women occasionally behave with levity in church, often do not attend well, and often are hard to manage; and that it is generally difficult to maintain harmony when there are women in a choir. And some believe that women are prohibited in the Bible from singing in church choirs.

Those who contend for the great musical capabilities of boys and their superiority to women, point to the singing in cathedrals, which they declare is 'most magnificent.' Doubtless at many cathedrals and collegiate churches which have choirschools attached to them, and at some very important parish churches, the boys sometimes sing excellently. But this, while it shows that boys may be effective singers when all the conditions are extremely favourable, does not prove them to be better singers than trained women. And the perfected singing of boys is not (cannot be) heard at most parish churches. The cathedral authorities are able to get good voices and keep up the succession, and the boys are trained and taught the elements of music by specialists, who understand their work, and can give ample time to it. The boys sing twice daily, and are always receiving instruction. They know that it is to their interest to make progress in music; and as they receive a free education and enjoy other advantages, they can be made to behave themselves. But all this is very different at the great majority of churches in country towns, where, as the conditions are less favourable, the singing is less satisfactory. Still less in villages does one expect to hear good singing by boys. And yet even in little villages chorister boys have made their appearance — the advocates for them apparently believing that boys with good voices are plentiful everywhere, and that capable trainers, who understand voice production and can teach singing, are to be found in every town and village in England. Strange delusion! In truth, boys with good voices are very scarce, and trainers with sufficient skill and patience to make boys of the ordinary type sing even tolerably, are still rarer. Moreover, boys need daily practice. But it would be hardly possible to get them to come to practice every day, or to persuade their parents to send them, unless they were well paid, and it were very much to their worldly advantage to do so. But if good material were obtainable, and the boys were practiced daily, and it were possible to secure the services of an able trainer, and such a person succeeded in developing their voices and teaching them their rudiments, no one could be sure that the boys would sing carefully, and their performance be tasteful and expressive.

Those who, while preferring the singing of women to that of boys, dislike to see women in the chancel (which they hold to be the proper place for the choir) are probably a numerous class. They think that the presence of the female element in the chancel is a violation of ecclesiastical propriety. No doubt the appearance in the chancel of a number of very gaily dressed women in objectionable; and attempts have been made to meet the difficulty (for it is a difficulty) by some who, knowing the superiority of women singers, have determined to retain them. Attempts have been made, and successfully in some places, to get all the women to wear dresses and bonnets of some plain colour. However, the presence of modest and quietly dressed women in the chancel does not seem objectionable.[a] If the choir occupied the west gallery — and there is no reason why it should not — it would not matter how the women were dressed.

The objection of women singers on the ground that the quality of the female voice renders it less fit for use in the Church services than boys' voices, is surely mere prejudice. The opinion that female voices impart a sensuous colouring to the music is too absurd to need refuting. Women's voices are indeed different as to tone-quality from boys', being less cold and penetrating, but fuller and more melodious. The writer recently heard a lady amateur say that she could listen with delight to the singing of a great soprano in oratorio, but would not like to hear her sing in church, because the female voice in church does not harmonize with the surroundings. And there are some who, while they hold that

---

[a] The writer is informed that at Roman Catholic churches the women, when the choir is in the chancel, are concealed by curtains or a screen of some kind. Those who, for any reason, dislike to see women singers in the chancel might copy this arrangement.

female voices ought not to be admitted into church choirs, kindly permit women to sing on festival occasions. With every desire to be candid, it is difficult to consider such opinions as these. It is surely a strange fancy that 'I know that my Redeemer' must not be sung in church unless a boy sings it — that while a singer of the first rank may, with propriety, sing this sublime air at the Albert Hall, she may not sing it in church, because her voice, by reason of its tone-quality, is not in harmony with the surroundings. And it is equally hard to believe that there is something so unchurchlike and profane in the quality of the female voice, that the choral singing of women, which delights us at musical festivals, so far from having a beautiful effect in church, sounds so much out of place in the sacred building that it must be banished therefrom at any cost.

The objection to women singers on the ground of levity, irregular attendance, and the difficulty of managing them and maintaining harmony among them is indeed a serious objection. Levity during Divine Service is an abomination that must be stopped, though sometimes it requires great tact to stop it. Probably most, if not all, women could attend well if they would. The writer knew a young woman, an excellent singer, who for seven years never missed a practice or a service when she was well and at home. But there is sometimes difficulty in getting careless and conceited women to attend well, though if an organist has influence he may do much to persuade. It generally happens in voluntary choirs where women are employed that some of them are hard to manage. The best singers, alas! are often conceited and impatient of correction. Easily offended themselves, they often sorely try the temper of the organist; and their jealousies and quarrelings — *Tantaene animis coelestibus irae?* — sometimes become a source of great trouble to him. Indeed, to control a voluntary choir, if there are many conceited or unamiable women in it, and to maintain harmony — nay, even to prevent a total disruption — requires very great tact and patience; and it has sometimes even been necessary to dismiss the more obstreperous females, if indeed their fancied wrongs have not already prompted them to leave of their own accord. These difficulties, however, hardly exist in choirs where the females are well-bred women, or some of the best singers are paid.

.   .   .   .

The following are the principal facts to be borne in mind in connection with our subject. Some women singers (the unamiable and conceited) are often troublesome, and require great tact to manage; a number of boys together are always very troublesome. Women are reliable; boys, because they are boys, are seldom to be depended on. Women may be trusted even with florid music (as anthems); boys sometimes fail in the simplest psalmody. With women for his supporters, an organist need know no fear; boys may go wrong any moment, and they are therefore a source of anxiety to clergymen Women with good voices are, in most places, easily procurable and need no great amount of teaching; boys with good voices are scarce and require endless labour to teach, and competent trainers are wanting. Women repay instruction, and generally sing excellently — often exquisitely; much valuable time and labour are often thrown away in teaching boys, and they seldom sing tolerably — often vilely.[b]

Though it is at present the fashion to remove women singers from choirs and substitute boys for them, choirs have not been improved, or the cause of Church music advanced, by the change. Those who have introduced the boy element into their choirs, can perhaps hardly be expected to confess that they have made a mistake. And many people, even if they notice the falling-off in Church music, regard it with little concern. But there are others who observe the degeneracy of Church choir singing, and know the cause of it; and these look forward to the day — and it will surely come — when the present fashion will give place to a better one, and women's voices (the most perfect and beautiful of all musical material) once more help to lead the praises of God in the sanctuary.

---

[b] The worthlessness of boys is generally very perceptible in their response-singing. In the Litany especially, where music, if employed at all, should be perfectly rendered, their false intonation is very marked.

Sir Charles Villiers Stanford

(1852-1924)

English composers of the last half of the nineteenth century who lived into the twentieth seldom devoted more than a fraction of their time to producing church music. Parry, Elgar, Stanford, and even Sullivan, who barely survived to the twentieth century, are among the great names of the period. Their interest in secular music did not seem to divorce them entirely from the area of church music; each contributed something of value. Stanford's vigorous interest in the quality of church music is apparent from his essay that follows.

Music in Cathedral and Church Choirs[1]

(A paper read before the Church Congress in London in 1899)

The Church is in a unique position as regards music. Music is, of all the arts, the one which is in the closest daily relationship with her. She is not dependent upon it for monetary profit, and, therefore, has a free hand in advancing what is best without regard to what will pay; a consideration which, in the circles of music itself, is unfortunately at all times a pressing problem. I take it that no one will deny that amongst the many duties of the Church, education, refinement, and improvement in matters of taste are not, or should not be, absent, and, therefore, I hold that in respect of music, it is not only possible, but imperative, that the Church should educate, refine, and improve its members in that particular branch of it which is especially devoted to herself. She should lead taste, and not follow it. She should uncompromisingly adopt what is best, irrespective of popularity, and eschew the second-rate, even if it is momentarily attractive. I am thus brought face to face with the question whether the Church, through her cathedrals and in "choirs and places where

---

[1]C. V. Stanford, *Studies and Memories* (London: Archibald Constable and Co. Ltd., 1908), pp. 61-69. Reprinted by permission of Constable and Company, Limited.

they sing," is doing her duty in this respect: and study of her recent musical records obliges me to answer the question with a decided negative.

Cathedral music in England has a great history. We have to thank the cathedrals for keeping alive, in artistically dark times, much of the half-buried talent of this country. They were the nurseries of such men as Tallis, Byrd, Gibbons, Farrant, and, greatest of all, Henry Purcell. The traditions of these men, and many more, are not lightly to be brushed aside. They represented not merely learning, but luminous fancy; their works were English to the backbone, solid in foundation; sometimes, perhaps, severe to a new acquaintance, but, once understood, always growing in sympathetic feeling, and constant in the affection they inspired. They have an atmosphere about them which affects every man who, from his childhood, has known an English cathedral. In this respect they occupy the same position in the English Church that Heinrich Schutz and the Bachs did in the Lutheran, and Palestrina and his contemporaries in the Roman.

At the present time, in the Roman Church, we find all the signs pointing in the direction of the renaissance of Palestrina and his school in connection with its services, and a general feeling to encourage the writing of sacred music on their lines. In the Lutheran Church the influence of Bach has never been superseded; it is as great now as ever it was, and even growing in influence. In the English alone do we find our own great masters being more and more systematically neglected, and a new conglomerate style introduce Talent, indeed, is not absent; it could scarcely be so in an age when music has made such strides in this country. There is plenty of good work to be found both among the elders and youngsters of these times; but, as in everything else, the best work is the rarest and the most difficult to sift from a mass of mediocrity, much •of which is not even grammatically written, much of which is veneered, tinselly, empty of idea, and some simply imported from sources, foreign in more senses than one, foreign to our buildings, to our services, and to our tastes. And this retrograde movement is of comparatively recent date. In the time of Samuel Wesley it was not so; his son, Samuel Sebastian Wesley, though he had a touch of the reformer in him, never led or hinted at revolution. Thomas Attwood Walmisley, one of the most gifted of our Church composers, never left the paths of the genuine school; Sterndale Bennett, though owing so much to German training and influence, never ceased to belong to the British school in his Church music, and had the deepest contempt for the undignified work of which he lived long enough to see the beginnings. If he had studied the recent records of our cathedral choirs, he would probably have despaired of the republic.

For the rapidly increasing elimination of the works of our old masters from the lists means the destruction of all history and tradition, and the undermining of taste. While other countries are not only preserving their great works, but by research adding those which have dropped out or been forgotten to their stores, we are locking up and forgetting volumes of treasures, and retaining for use only a few of the most obvious and best known. I will give you a very few of the most glaring instances, which I have obtained from a record of the music given in fifty-one of our cathedrals and collegiate churches. Purcell's 'Evening Service' in G Minor, one of the very finest works we possess, appears only in eight lists; on the other hand, a modern service of wonderful vapidity, which shall be nameless, appears in thirty-four. Gibbons' magnificent anthem, 'O Thou, the central orb,' appears only in three; S. S. Wesley's finest work, 'Let us lift up our heart,' in four; Walmisley's best anthem, 'If the Lord Himself,' in ten; while a vulgar modern anthem of foreign origin is given in thirty-one places. I have observed also the relative value given to foreign composers. Palestrina receives but forty performances of seventeen works, and is recognised only in eighteen cathedrals; Sebastian Bach, the greatest of all, and the most in sympathy with our tastes and traditions, received but ninety-nine performances in twenty-six cathedrals of his innumerable masterpieces. While, on the other hand, a modern foreign composer, alien to our style, and representing all that is most empty, showy, and superficial in religious music, gets two hundred and thirty-one performances of thirty-three anthems in no less than forty-four of our cathedrals. The net result of the record I have studied shows that the proportion of works given is five modern to one ancient. A lamentable history this. As well might we bring up the children of our age upon three-volume novels, providing them with five sensational books for every one of serious or solid value.

What is the cause of this condition of affairs? Partly, perhaps, a lack of veneration of our traditions, which is not lacking also in other directions at the end of this nineteenth century. Partly the fact that music has become so popular, and has been studied so much more widely in recent years, that the supply has not been limited to the works of those who have something to say and know how to say it; and many ambitious pens, who have not attained to sufficient mastery to be able to write a movement in form, have been led to attempt the shorter, more scrappy, and (apparently) more easy method of setting the canticles or writing a short anthem.

But the real root of the mischief is, I am convinced, the trammelled position of the man who is responsible for the performance of the music, and who is, perhaps, in many cathedral bodies the only representative of thoroughly trained knowledge of the subject—the organist. In most cases the responsibility for the choice of music is not centred in him, the expert, but either altogether in the hands of the clergy, or divided between a precentor and the organist. There are, of course, instances where this disastrous policy does not hold, and very striking instances too; but they are unfortunately exceptions, not rules. Division of responsibility, or the assignment of it to the non-expert is alike, to my mind, a fatal mistake. Like most other matters of a like nature, this custom is a survival of ancient time, when the conditions were wholly different. Formerly the monk was a more learned and cultivated musician than his servant, the organist or choir-trainer. He therefore rightly dictated the choice of music, of which he was a master. The positions are now reversed. The organist is the learned and cultivated musician, and the clerical official has not (save in a very few instances) qualified either by study or research for a task demanding exceptional musical skill and routine. But he retains a power for which he has in the lapse of time lost the necessary equipment, and the result is a far-spread amateurishness of taste, which if it is permitted to rule, will inevitably destroy the best traditions of English Church music. Moreover, the organist, aware beforehand that he will have little or no control over the music to be given, is thus discouraged from studying seriously the history and literature, as well as the technique of his branch of the art. What would be said if an organist claimed control over the subjects and tendencies of the sermons to be delivered by the clergy? The suggestion seems ridiculous, but it is not one whit more so than the condition of affairs which I have described.

I am not speaking of these matters merely from hearsay, but also from personal experience. I was for many years an organist. I venture, therefore, to recount, as shortly as possible, my own experiences. When I entered upon my duties, I found that the choice of all the music was made by the precentor. To this choice I was expected to sign my name with his. But when I found that I had practically no voice either in insertion or elimination, I declined to append my name to a list of music with the selection of which I had nothing to do. For many years, although the university to which I had the honour to belong had thought me worthy in knowledge and experience of being elected to their Professorship of Music, in my own College Chapel I was absolutely powerless to control or direct the choice of works which were to influence the tastes of hundred of students. Surely such a policy is mischievous. Needless to say that the result of it was that many generations of young Englishmen left their college without knowing the greatest and best of the works of the English Cathedral School; works which, even when I was a youth, were the daily bread of all who went to a choral service. I have heard Purcell termed dull, Gibbons dry, and known their finest anthems obliterated from the lists after one hearing, because they were not (to use the ready terms of the day) sufficiently 'bright and attractive': terms for which I venture to substitute 'superficial and hysterical.'

If, then, such conditions as these are to prevail much longer in our cathedral and church choirs, we may say good-bye to the great store of noble music which our musical forefathers have bequeathed to us. We shall find put in its place flimsy and ephemeral trivialities, which have just enough sensationalism in them to tickle the musical palate; we shall find music, much of it excellent in its proper place, but written for totally different conditions in other countries, imported into our services, destroying their character, and altering the whole taste of the community; a taste which it has taken seven centuries to build up in this country. Take, for instance, the adaptation of the Masses of Haydn, Mozart, or Schubert to the English Communion Service. No one admires them more than I do, but what treatment has to be meted out to them? A Mass, as written for the Roman ritual, is a thought-out and balanced piece of work, not merely scraps of movements, which may be played in any order, but as homogeneous as any sonata or symphony. What would be thought if a conductor, in order to present the Eroica Symphony of Beethoven to an English audience, cut out three-fourths of the first movement, and played the second movement at the end as a Finale? Yet this is what is done with any adapted Mass in our English services. The Kyrie (for which there is no place) is cut down and mutilated for words to which it only very partially applies, and the Gloria, written to follow immediately after the Kyrie, is perforce removed from its place, and sung at the end of a work which was designed to finish with the Dona nobis pacem. This vandalism is being perpetrated somewhere every Sunday, and

the finest designs of the great foreign masters are mutilated after
the most drastic and Procrustean methods. If the old English
masters are to be disestablished, at any rate let their places be
taken by works appropriate for the purpose, and not by the
distortion of masterpieces which were written for other purposes.
The advice I would venture to give is best expressed in the words
of two great composers in this century. As Wagner says in the
Meistersinger, '*Ehrt eure deutschen Meister*,' so let me adapt it, 'Honour
your English Masters'; and as Verdi said not long ago, '*Torniamo
all' antico*,' make the mainstay of your music the great works of
the past, without ceasing to encourage and include all that is best
and most genuine in contemporary music. And leave the control of
the choice of music to the man whose life-work it is to study and
understand it, the man whom you put in command of your organ
and your choir. Pick the best artist you can, and when you have
put him in the post, leave him alone; and if he abuses his trust,
turn him out. But stop this hopeless method of either dividing
responsibility or placing it in the hands of the inexperienced
amateur.

THE TWENTIETH CENTURY

Pope Pius X

(1835-1914)

The most recent full-scale document devoted entirely to music of the Catholic Church was issued by Pope Pius X in the year he was elected to his high office. In addition to summing up the grievances of the past, it laid down firm guidelines for the future, clear, unequivocal, and liturgically authoritative. The restrictions that were imposed in that document were of such dimensions that the established practices of churches and choirs of all sizes were subject to complete revision; publishers were in danger of losing money on large inventories of music that did not fit the stipulations; church libraries were likewise overstocked with Masses and other pieces that were not permissible under the newly stated rules.

As early as its meeting of 1922, the Society of St. Gregory went on record with a Black List of unauthorized music, comprising Masses, hymnals, popularized airs, and works that had been hurriedly revised by publishers — by removing repetitions or nonliturgical sections — in order to circumvent the restrictions of the Motu Proprio.

On December 20, 1928, Pope Pius XI reaffirmed the provisions of the Motu Proprio in the Apostolic Constitution, "Divini Cultus Sanctitatem." Since those years we have seen the most drastic changes ever to overtake Catholic practice. Modifications of liturgical custom or language, however, are difficult to adjust to musical practice, and the Church is now undergoing an agonizing reappraisal in many ways. The freedoms of our time will probably never permit the issuance of another such restrictive document as the Motu Proprio, at least not with any hope of its uncontested wide acceptance. Many of the features specifically forbidden in 1903 are already commonly practiced. Printing the document here permits us to see the last strong stand taken by the Church; it does not in any way predict future practices or attitudes.

Motu Proprio of Pope Pius X on Sacred Music[1]
(November 22, 1903)

Among the cares of the pastoral office, not only of this

[1] *Papal Documents on Sacred Music*, pp. 7-10. Reprinted by permission of *Sacred Music*, Journal of The Church Music Association of America.

Supreme Chair, which We, though unworthy, occupy through the inscrutable disposition of Providence, but of every local church, a leading one is without question that of maintaining and promoting the decorum of the House of God in which the august mysteries of religion are celebrated, and where the Christian people assemble to receive the grace of the Sacraments, to assist at the Holy Sacrifice of the Altar, to adore the most august Sacrament of the Lord's Body and to unite in the common prayer of the Church in the public and solemn liturgical offices. Nothing should have place, therefore, in the temple calculated to disturb or even merely to diminish the piety and devotion of the faithful, nothing that may give reasonable cause for disgust or scandal, nothing, above all, which directly offends the decorum and sanctity of the sacred functions and is thus unworthy of the House of Prayer and of the Majesty of God. We do not touch separately on the abuses in this matter which may arise. Today Our attention is directed to one of the most common of them, one of the most difficult to eradicate, and the existence of which is sometimes to be deplored in places where everything else is deserving of the highest praise — the beauty and sumptuousness of the temple, the splendour and the accurate performance of the ceremonies, the attendance of the clergy, the gravity and piety of the officiating ministers. Such is the abuse affecting sacred chant and music. And indeed, whether it is owing to the very nature of this art, fluctuating and variable as it is in itself, or to the succeeding changes in tastes and habits with the course of time, or to the fatal influence exercised on the sacred art by profane and theatrical art, or to the pleasure that music directly produces, and that is not always easily contained within the right limits, or finally to the many prejudices on the matter, so lightly introduced and so tenaciously maintained even among responsible and pious persons, the fact remains that there is a general tendency to deviate from the right rule, prescribed by the end for which art is admitted to the service of public worship and which is set forth very clearly in the ecclesiastical Canons, in the Ordinances of the General and Provincial Councils, in the prescriptions which have at various times emanated from the Sacred Roman Congregations, and from Our Predecessors the Sovereign Pontiffs.

It is with real satisfaction that We acknowledge the large amount of good that has been effected in this respect during the last decade in this Our fostering city of Rome, and in many churches in Our country, but in a more especial way among some nations in which illustrious men, full of zeal for the worship of

God, have, with the approval of the Holy See and under the
direction of the Bishops, united in flourishing Societies and
restored sacred music to the fullest honour in all their churches
and chapels. Still the good work that has been done is very far
indeed from being common to all, and when We consult Our own
personal experience and take into account the great number of
complaints that have reached Us during the short time that has
elapsed since it pleased the Lord to elevate Our humility to the
supreme summit of the Roman Pontificate, We consider it Our
first duty, without further delay, to raise Our voice at once in
reproof and condemnation of all that is seen to be out of harmony
with the right rule above indicated, in the functions of public
worship and in the performance of the ecclesiastical offices. Filled
as We are with a most ardent desire to see the true Christian
spirit flourish in every respect and be preserved by all the faithful,
We deem it necessary to provide before aught else for the sanctity
and dignity of the temple, in which the faithful assemble for no
other object than that of acquiring this spirit from its foremost
and indispensable fount, which is the active participation in the
most holy mysteries and in the public and solemn prayer of the
Church. And it is vain to hope that the blessing of heaven will
descend abundantly upon us, when our homage to the Most High,
instead of ascending in the odor of sweetness, puts into the hand
of the Lord the scourges wherewith of old the Divine Redeemer
drove the unworthy profaners from the Temple.

Hence, in order that no one for the future may be able to plead
in excuse that he did not clearly understand his duty and that all
vagueness may be eliminated from the interpretation of matters
which have already been commanded, We have deemed it
expedient to point out briefly the principles regulating sacred
music in the functions of public worship, and to gather together
in a general survey the principal prescriptions of the Church
against the more common abuses in this subject. We do therefore
publish, *motu proprio* and with certain knowledge, Our present
Instruction to which, as a *juridical code of sacred music (quasi a codice
giuridice della musica sacra)*, We will with the fullness of Our
Apostolic Authority that the force of law be given, and We do by
Our present handwriting impose its scrupulous observance on all.

Instruction on Sacred Music
I
GENERAL PRINCIPLES

1. Sacred music, being a complementary part of the solemn liturgy, participates in the general scope of the liturgy, which is the glory of God and the sanctification and edification of the faithful. It contributes to the decorum and the splendor of the ecclesiastical ceremonies, and since its principal office is to clothe with suitable melody the liturgical text proposed for the understanding of the faithful, its proper aim is to add greater efficacy to the text, in order that through it the faithful may be the more easily moved to devotion and better disposed for the reception of the fruits of grace belonging to the celebration of the most holy mysteries.

2. Sacred music should consequently possess, in the highest degree, the qualities proper to the liturgy, and in particular *sanctity* and *goodness of form*, which will spontaneously produce the final quality of *universality*.

It must be *holy*, and must, therefore, exclude all profanity not only in itself, but in the manner in which it is presented by those who execute it.

It must be *true art*, for otherwise it will be impossible for it to exercise on the minds of those who listen to it that efficacy which the Church aims at obtaining in admitting into her liturgy the art of musical sounds.

But it must, at the same time, be *universal* in the sense that while every nation is permitted to admit into its ecclesiastical compositions those special forms which may be said to constitute its native music, still these forms must be subordinated in such a manner to the general characteristics of sacred music that nobody of any nation may receive an impression other than good on hearing them.

II
THE DIFFERENT KINDS OF SACRED MUSIC

3. These qualities are to be found, in the highest degree, in Gregorian Chant, which is, consequently, the Chant proper to the Roman Church, the only chant she has inherited from the ancient fathers, which she has jealously guarded for centuries in her liturgical codices, which she directly proposes to the faithful as her own, which she prescribes exclusively for some parts of the liturgy,

and which the most recent studies have so happily restored to their integrity and purity.

On these grounds Gregorian Chant has always been regarded as the supreme model for sacred music, so that it is fully legitimate to lay down the following rule: *the more closely a composition for church approaches in its movement, inspiration and savor the Gregorian form, the more sacred and liturgical it becomes; and the more out of harmony it is with that supreme model, the less worthy it is of the temple.*

The ancient traditional Gregorian Chant must, therefore, in a large measure be restored to the functions of public worship, and the fact must be accepted by all that an ecclesiastical function loses none of its solemnity when accompanied by this music alone.

Special efforts are to be made to restore the use of the Gregorian Chant by the people, so that the faithful may again take a more active part in the ecclesiastical offices, as was the case in ancient times.

4. The above-mentioned qualities are also possessed in an excellent degree by Classic Polyphony, especially of the Roman School, which reached its greatest perfection in the fifteenth [sixteenth] century, owing to the works of Pierluigi da Palestrina, and continued subsequently to produce compositions of excellent quality from a liturgical and musical standpoint. Classic Polyphony agrees admirably with Gregorian Chant, the supreme model of all sacred music, and hence it has been found worthy of a place side by side with Gregorian Chant, in the more solemn functions of the Church, such as those of the Pontifical Chapel. This, too, must therefore be restored largely in ecclesiastical functions, especially in the more important basilicas, in cathedrals, and in the churches and chapels of seminaries and other ecclesiastical institutions in which the necessary means are usually not lacking.

5. The Church has always recognized and favoured the progress of the arts, admitting to the service of religion everything good and beautiful discovered by genius in the course of ages — always, however, with due regard to the liturgical laws. Consequently modern music is also admitted to the Church, since it, too, furnishes compositions of such excellence, sobriety and gravity, that they are in no way unworthy of the liturgical functions.

Still, since modern music has risen mainly to serve profane uses, greater care must be taken with regard to it, in order that the musical compositions of modern style which are admitted in the Church may contain nothing profane, be free from reminiscences of motifs adopted in the theatres, and be not fashioned even in their external forms after the manner of profane pieces.

6. Among the different kinds of modern music, that which appears less suitable for accompanying the functions of public worship is the theatrical style, which was in the greatest vogue, especially in Italy, during the last century. This of its very nature is diametrically opposed to Gregorian Chant and classic polyphony, and therefore to the most important law of all good sacred music. Besides the intrinsic structure, the rhythm and what is known as the *conventionalism* of this style adapt themselves but badly to the requirements of true liturgical music.

III
THE LITURGICAL TEXT

7. The language proper to the Roman Church is Latin. Hence it is forbidden to sing anything whatever in the vernacular in solemn liturgical functions — much more to sing in the vernacular the variable or common parts of the Mass and Office.

8. As the texts that may be rendered in music, and the order in which they are to be rendered, are determined for every liturgical function, it is not lawful to confuse this order or to change the prescribed texts for others selected at will, or to omit them entirely or even in part, unless when the rubrics allow that some versicles of the text be supplied with the organ, while these versicles are simply recited in the choir. However, it is permissible, according to the custom of the Roman Church, to sing a motet to the Blessed Sacrament after the *Benedictus* in a Solemn Mass. It is also permitted, after the Offertory prescribed for the Mass has been sung, to execute during the time that remains a brief motet to words approved by the Church.

9. The liturgical text must be sung as it is in the books, without alteration or inversion of the words, without undue repetition, without breaking syllables, and always in a manner intelligible to the faithful who listen.

IV
EXTERNAL FORM OF THE SACRED COMPOSITIONS

10. The different parts of the Mass and the Office must retain, even musically, that particular concept and form which ecclesiastical tradition has assigned to them, and which is admirably brought out by Gregorian Chant. The method of composing an *introit*, a *gradual*, an *antiphon*, a *psalm*, a *hymn*, a *Gloria in excelsis*, etc., must therefore be distinct from one another.

11. In particular the following rules are to be observed:

(a) The *Kyrie, Gloria, Credo,* etc., of the Mass must preserve the unity of composition proper to their text. It is not lawful, therefore, to compose them in separate movements, in such a way that each of these movements form a complete composition in itself, and be capable of being detached from the rest and substituted by another.

(b) In the office of Vespers it should be the rule to follow the *Caeremoniale Episcoporum,* which prescribes Gregorian Chant for the psalmody and permits figured music for the versicles of the *Gloria Patri* and the hymn.

It will nevertheless be lawful on greater solemnities to alternate the Gregorian Chant of the choir with the so-called *falsi-bordoni* or with verses similarly composed in a proper manner.

It is also permissible occasionally to render single psalms in their entirety in music, provided the form proper to psalmody be preserved in such compositions; that is to say, provided the singers seem to be psalmodising among themselves either with new motifs or with those taken from Gregorian Chant or based upon it.

The psalms known as *di concerto* are therefore forever excluded and prohibited.

(c) In the hymns of the Church the traditional form of the hymn is preserved. It is not lawful, therefore, to compose, for instance, a *Tantum ergo* in such wise that the first strophe presents a romanza, a cavatina, an adagio and the *Genitori* an allegro.

(d) The antiphons of the Vespers must be as a rule rendered with the Gregorian melody proper to each. Should they, however, in some special case be sung in figured music, they must never have either the form of a concert melody or the fullness of a motet or a cantata.

V

THE SINGERS

12. With the exception of the melodies proper to the celebrant at the altar and to the ministers, which must be always sung in Gregorian Chant, and without accompaniment of the organ, all the rest of the liturgical chant belongs to the choir of levites, and, therefore, singers in church, even when they are laymen, are really taking the place of the ecclesiastical choir. Hence the music rendered by them must, at least for the greater part, retain the character of choral music.

By this it is not to be understood that solos are entirely

excluded. But solo singing should never predominate to such an extent as to have the greater part of the liturgical chant executed in that manner; the solo phrase should have the character or hint of a melodic projection *(spunto),* and be strictly bound up with the rest of the choral composition.

13. On the same principle it follows that singers in church have a real liturgical office, and that therefore women, being incapable of exercising such office, cannot be admitted to form part of the choir. Whenever, then, it is desired to employ the acute voices of sopranos and contraltos, these parts must be taken by boys, according to the most ancient usage of the Church.

14. Finally, only men of known piety and probity of life are to be admitted to form part of the choir of a church, and these men should by their modest and devout bearing during the liturgical functions show that they are worthy of the holy office they exercise. It will also be fitting that singers while singing in church wear the ecclesiastical habit and surplice, and that they be hidden behind gratings when the choir is excessively open to the public gaze.

VI
ORGAN AND INSTRUMENTS

15. Although the music proper to the Church is purely vocal music, music with the accompaniment of the organ is also permitted. In some special cases, within due limits and with proper safeguards, other instruments may be allowed, but never without the special permission of the Ordinary, according to prescriptions of the *Caeremoniale Episcoporum.*

16. As the singing should always have the principal place, the organ or other instrument should merely sustain and never oppress it.

17. It is not permitted to have the chant preceded by long preludes or to interrupt it with intermezzo pieces.

18. The sound of the organ as an accompaniment to the chant in preludes, interludes, and the like must be not only governed by the special nature of the instrument, but must participate in all the qualities proper to sacred music as above enumerated.

19. The employment of the piano is forbidden in church, as is also that of noisy or frivolous instruments such as drums, cymbals, bells and the like.

20. It is strictly forbidden to have bands play in church, and only in special cases with the consent of the Ordinary will it be

permissible to admit wind instruments, limited in number, judiciously used, and proportioned to the size of the place — provided the composition and accompaniment be written in grave and suitable style, and conform in all respects to that proper to the organ.

21. In processions outside the church the Ordinary may give permission for a band, provided no profane pieces be executed. It would be desirable in such cases that the band confine itself to accompanying some spiritual canticle sung in Latin or in the vernacular by the singers and the pious associations which take part in the procession.

VII
THE LENGTH OF THE LITURGICAL CHANT

22. It is not lawful to keep the priest at the altar waiting on account of the chant or the music for a length of time not allowed for by the liturgy. According to the ecclesiastical prescriptions the *Sanctus* of the Mass should be over before the elevation, and therefore the priest must here have regard for the singers. The *Gloria* and the *Credo* ought, according to the Gregorian tradition, to be relatively short.

23. In general it must be considered a very grave abuse when the liturgy in ecclesiastical functions is made to appear secondary to and in a manner at the service of the music, for the music is merely a part of the liturgy and its humble handmaid.

VIII
PRINCIPAL MEANS

24. For the exact execution of what has been herein laid down, the Bishops, if they have not already done so, are to institute in their dioceses a special Commission composed of persons really competent in sacred music, and to this Commission let them entrust in the manner they find most suitable the task of watching over the music executed in their churches. Nor are they to see merely that the music is good in itself, but also that it is adapted to the power of the singers and be always well executed.

25. In seminaries of clerics and in ecclesiastical institutions let the above-mentioned traditional Gregorian Chant be cultivated by all with diligence and love, according to the Tridentine prescriptions, and let the superiors be liberal of encouragement and praise toward their young subjects. In like manner let a 'Schola

Cantorum be established, whenever possible, among the clerics for the execution of sacred polyphony and of good liturgical music.

26. In the ordinary lessons of Liturgy, Morals, Canon Law given to the students of theology, let care be taken to touch on those points which regard more directly the principles and laws of sacred music, and let an attempt be made to complete the doctrine with some particular instruction in the aesthetic side of sacred art, so that the clerics may not leave the seminary ignorant of all those subjects so necessary to a full ecclesiastical education.

27. Let care be taken to restore, at least in the principal churches, the ancient *Scholae Cantorum*. as has been done with excellent fruit in a great many places. It is not difficult for a zealous clergy to institute such *Scholae* even in smaller churches and country parishes — nay, in these last the pastors will find a very easy means of gathering around them both children and adults, to their own profit and the edification of the people.

28. Let efforts be made to support and promote, in the best way possible, the higher schools of sacred music where these already exist, and to help in founding them where they do not. Its of the utmost importance that the Church herself provide for the instruction of her choirmasters, organists, and singers according to the true principles of sacred art.

IX
CONCLUSION

29. Finally, it is recommended to choirmasters, singers, members of the clergy, superiors of seminaries, ecclesiastical institutions, and religious communities, parish priests and rectors of churches, canons of collegiate churches and cathedrals, and, above all, to the diocesan ordinaries to favor with all zeal these prudent reforms, long desired and demanded with united voice by all; so that the authority of the Church, which herself has repeatedly proposed them, and now inculcates them, may not fall into contempt.

Given from Our Apostolic Palace at the Vatican, on day of the Virgin and Martyr, St. Cecilia, November 22, 1903, in the first year of Our Pontificate.

PIUS X, POPE

O. G. T. Sonneck

(1873-1928)

In the first quarter of this century, Sonneck was one of the most influential forces in American music except for its performers and composers. As Chief of the Music Division of the Library of Congress, and later as the first editor of *The Musical Quarterly*, he was heard with respect. He left a considerable body of published material, much of it dealing with American music. It is significant, then, that he shared in — and possibly helped to continue — the low opinion that was held of American church music in his paper, "A Survey of Music in America," read before a musical society in New York two years before the *Quarterly* was founded in 1915. [1]

The temptation to survey church-music in America I can resist with ease. Abstinence from churchly habits unfits me for intelligent utterance on the subject. That there is room for reforms is clear, otherwise pens and typewriters would not be kept busy demanding and suggesting reforms. Whether or not the church is still often looked upon by many church-goers as a kind of concert-hall with liturgy, sermons, prayers, etc., thrown in, where one can hear music excellently performed and practically for nothing, I am not prepared to say. If that still be the case, those engaged in subordinating the charms of music to the dignity of Divine Service have my heartfelt sympathy. My impression is that things are not nearly so bad as they used to be. The pendulum seems to be swinging from mere music in churches to more churchly music. With this impression uppermost in my mind, I prefer to look on such a program as I happen to have on my desk at home as a mere freakish curiosity. The program is that of a musical evening service in a fashionable church, and one-half of it

---

[1] Privately printed in 1913, the entire essay was later made a part of a volume of Sonneck's essays: O. G. Sonneck, *Suum Cuique: Essays in Music* (New York: G. Schirmer, 1916). The passage quoted here appears on pages 125-26 of that volume.

consists of anthems by one Richard Wagner — yes, anthems by Richard Wagner, or rather selections from his operas designated as anthems after the substitution of sacred English words for the original secular German. Add to that "processional marches" arranged for the organ from his operas, and you will know my reason for not going to church on that occasion, at least.

Archibald T. Davison

(1883-1961)

American scholars who have addressed themselves seriously to the matter of church music are not numerous. Among those who have recently done so, the emphasis has been on history rather than practice. On at least two occasions, however, A. T. Davison considered procedures and propriety rather than the development of the genre. The section from this, his earlier volume (which first appeared in 1920), is part of a chapter entitled "Attitudes and Conditions Affecting Protestant Church Music." After half a century, and despite many changes of style in dogma and music, it is still pertinent.

Individualism[1]

If only there were some imminent likelihood that the indifferent and complacent would awaken to the responsibility that is theirs to improve education for the benefit of church music, a long step forward would have been taken. But unfortunately quite the reverse is the case. Take the layman, for example, the most powerful factor in the problem. He is in a position to dictate the course of church music because he is numerically superior and he pays the bills. He says he doesn't know much about music (by which he means that he does not play the piano) but he knows what pleases him. And if you tell him that the church music he likes is not only bad music but profane as well and that he is guilty of near-sacrilege in countenancing its performance, he becomes very indignant, as any good American would, and says he doesn't consider it anybody's business what his taste is and he doesn't propose to let a high-brow tell him what he ought or ought not to prefer; the music suits him, it makes him feel good, and that's enough.

We live in an age of individualism where art occupies a place

---

[1] Archibald T. Davison, *Protestant Church Music in America* (Boston: E. C. Schirmer Music Co., 1933), pp. 26-32. Copyright, 1933, by E. C. Schirmer Music Co. Used with permission.

remote from the significance and dignity which was bestowed upon it by older civilizations. Since the war, striking examples of our individualistic attitude toward all branches of art appear from time to time, and in order to prevent the committing of artistic atrocities, many municipalities now require that all memorials such as fountains, monuments, tablets, and the like, shall be passed upon by a jury of art experts before the object in question shall be permanently installed. Then come loud cries from prospective donors, defiant utterances, appeals to the ideal of personal liberty, the spirit of '76, or what not. All this is quite sincere, for the average man is unable to understand why his munificence should be subject to restriction since his gift can make no *physical* difference to anyone. He may be willing to labor in behalf of good public morals, education (in the categorical sense), hygiene, or public utilities, but he does not perceive that his failure to appreciate the importance of a community standard of beauty constitutes an arraignment of his own public spirit. Popularly speaking, music is a by-product of activity and not an end in itself. It will be many a day, I fear, before Americans generally perceive that beauty is, indeed, an integral part of the moral order; and I am sure that it would be difficult, or even impossible, at present to persuade the American layman that his tolerance of unworthy music in church or elsewhere constitutes an offence either against society or against God.

Individualism among church musicians arises generally from a narrow or limited musical training. I can think of but few musicians, who, having been exposed to good church music over a period of years, deliberately threw away their talents on the cheap and the mediocre. To pronounce them opportunists would be uncharitable. They are, perhaps, sufferers from paralysis of the discriminatory function; musicians who are congenitally incapable of perceiving what is good and what is bad. Yet there are others whose gifts are not thus limited who have no desire to educate themselves or to strive for the establishment of healthier church music conditions. Like the layman who resents any imputation of inferiority in aesthetic outlook, the church musician generally stiffens against any suggestion that there is a better musical country beyond. He too refers to 'highbrow' and 'theoretical' opinion, and closes the argument with the flat assertion that never having lost a church job he'll back his opinion against anyone's. Again, condemnation must not be universal. In growing numbers of American churches are musicians, well-educated and endowed with a sense of responsibility, who are the prophets of a better day. As church music enlightenment advances their ranks will inevitably and happily increase.

Many clergymen tend to judge the quality of church music by its effect upon their pulpit efficiency. This is natural but unfortunate since it leads to the application of principles in no way relating to the case, particularly where clerical displeasure centers on performance. Sloppy organ playing or indifferent singing may well affect a man's preaching, but this is, in reality, a superficial consideration. Surely it is not the function of church music to supply the minister with inspiration. The best church music is capable of doing just that, but whether it succeeds or not depends   not on its character or performance but upon the clergyman himself. Incidentally no greater slight may be cast upon the dignity of church music or upon the sincerity of the musicians than to praise in public either music or performance. By the same token the most eloquent tribute to the complete effectiveness of noble church music which I have ever witnessed befell after a none too smooth performance of Byrd's "The souls of the righteous," when a clergyman of rare discernment, evidently much moved and sensing the fact that after such transcendent music, however performed, any spoken word would forever destroy a moment of unearthly serenity, forebore to read the prescribed lesson and knelt in silent prayer. This man, for once at least, had borne in upon him the fundamental fact that the question of good or bad church music is settled not by *means* but by *substance.* What constitutes appropriateness of substance is too often determined, however, by the personal preference of the individual for a certain type of music quite apart from its technical make-up and the associations which surround it, or by confused thinking which embraces almost any type of music as eligible to be included within the category of 'church music.' Perhaps the most striking example of tangled opinion on this matter comes from Liszt, who, speaking for himself and Berlioz, said: "For want of a better term we may well call the new music Humanitarian. It must be devotional, strong, and drastic, uniting — on a colossal scale — the theatre and the church, dramatic and sacred, superb and simple, fiery and free, strong and calm, translucent and emotional."[a] The man who declared "Wagner is my religion" was less inclusive but equally muddled, for the associations that group themselves about Wagner's music — associations arising from the secular quality of the text and from the conditions under which the music is

---

[a] *Gazette Musicale,* 1834, quoted in *The Oxford History of Music* (Vol. VI).

properly heard — are definitely secular and even theatrical. No composer, moreover, has succeeded better in supporting his text with a musical fabric of the most intensely emotional and perhaps erotic kind.

When we are in a position to impose our preferences on others the situation becomes dangerous, particularly because those preferences are generally dictated by purely emotional reactions to the music. Let us, for the moment, assume our Wagnerian enthusiast to be a parson or a music committeeman; he may, of course, insist upon the performance of Wagner at Sunday services but if he is wise with a knowledge of the infinitely variable emotional appeal of music, he will say, "I have the greatest admiration for Wagner and he supplies for me what seem to be spiritual stimuli. On the other hand his music may, and probably does have quite a different effect upon others. Therefore, while I shall permit myself the privilege of interpreting Wagner's music as sacred whenever I hear it, in view of its secular connotations I cannot conscientiously recommend it as church music." Dogmatizing about what is good or bad church music is permissible only when supported by extensive technical equipment or reasoned theory.

Again individualism becomes rampant when there is a denominational hymn-book to be compiled. More than one editor has told me of receiving letters from clergymen reading, "I *demand* that you include the music of such and such hymns in our church hymnal." What right has anyone, it may justly be asked, to place upon an editor limitations which may result in the exclusion of material more general in application and better for congregational singing than the particular object of some minister's musical fancy?

Tolerance walks humbly before knowledge and we must hope for broadmindedness, at least until such time as those in whose hands the administration of church music is vested shall have received an education adequate to fit them for their responsibilities.

H. C. Colles

(1879-1943)

At various times a teacher, performer, critic, and editor, H. C. Colles was sufficiently informed and experienced to hold forth at length about church music. That only a small portion of his extensive output was devoted to the discussion of such music shows the subordinate place it has taken in the thoughts of scholars and critics, not only in England but in the entire world of music. The brief essay quoted here pithily states what many others have taken much more space to discuss.

"Church Music," 22 July 1922.[1]

I confess myself reluctant to embark on the subject of Church music. It has been the cause of so much dissension, and advice has been poured out so liberally on those responsible for it by those who have no responsibility in the matter, that one fears to add to the confusion. Besides, it is obvious that so many considerations come into play here which have little to do with any artistic problem, traditions and associations, religious convictions and dearly held prejudices, that the wayfaring man may be no great fool and yet err therein. But the difficulties of the subject are, in truth, merely an indication that Church music is more of a human problem than many another question of art can claim to be, at any rate in this country.

The other day a leading article in *The Times* drew attention to the committee recently appointed by the Archbishops to conduct an inquiry into the state of Church music and the fact provides a starting point. It limits the scope to the special problem of the Church of England, and, even so, the problem is still more than large enough to fill the space available for its consideration here. Let us draw the limits closer still, and realize that there is a

---

[1]H. C. Colles, *Essays and Lectures* (London: Humphrey Milford; Oxford University Press, 1945), pp. 136-37. Reprinted by kind permission of H. G. Matheson, copyright owner.

distinction between Church music and music in church.

At the present day, churches of all kinds are used for the performance of all sorts of music which is not strictly church music. There seems to be a fairly general agreement that this is legitimate and desirable, and such uses of the churches range from the festivals of the Three Choirs to performances of cantatas and similar works by the choirs of village churches. But this is not Church music. The parson merely stipulates that it shall be associated with words or ideas, at any rate, not too widely divergent from the ideals of the Christian religion.

A canon of Hereford last year pointed out to me with evident satisfaction that one festival programme had ranged from the Latin "Stabat Mater" to the Gnostic "Hymn of Jesus", and thence by way of Goethe's Pantheism (as set by Brahms) to Blake's denunciation of orthodoxy under figure of the "wheel of Religion". Probably the musicians who took part in it were serenely unaware that in the course of four hours or so they had thrown themselves whole-heartedly into a series of sentiments so widely incompatible with one another that no Church could pretend to embrace them and remain a Church at all. They were artistically perfectly compatible, because each one of the works was the genuine expression of a sincere artistic conviction. This is all that the artist demands of concert music, whether it takes place in a cathedral or a Concert Hall, and most churchmen are agreed that artistic seriousness is a sufficient passport to the cathedral on such occasions as these.

But a different standard must obtain where the services of the Church are concerned, and one of the difficulties of the present time is that many church musicians do not appreciate that standard or realize that it needs an appropriate expression in music. I have recently heard musicians talk as though a commission to report on the needs of Church music were a commission to effect drastic reforms of the Liturgy. It may be very desirable to reform the Liturgy; but whether that is so or not, it is no business of the musician as such. His business is the simpler one of finding the right music for the Liturgy which happens to be in use, and to do that he must begin by understanding it and sympathizing with its intention. If he cannot honestly do so, he must leave Church music, properly so-called, for some more congenial branch of his art.

James F. White

At the time the material quoted here was written, James F. White was a teacher of religion at Ohio Wesleyan University. The first half of his essay is devoted to the development of choirs from the time (1841) Walter F. Hook followed John Jebb's suggestion to employ the cathedral-style service in a new parish church in Leeds. His conclusions, concerned with the relationship between the choir and the congregation in the act of worship, are such as a musician would be reluctant to reach. The entire issue of *The Christian Century* from which this was taken was devoted to an appraisal of church music in that year. It is doubtful that the material printed there had any wide influence, but it is a significant indication of mid-century problems that a periodical not usually concerned with music should devote an entire number to that topic. Change in our time is so rapid that a similar review would be welcome each decade.

Excerpt from "Church Choir: Friend or Foe?"[1]

. . . .

No doubt many people would state that the real purpose of choral music is to add beauty to the service. Yet it is highly questionable whether the pursuit of beauty as an abstraction is either good art or good theology. Few if any great artists have deliberately tried to make their work beautiful. Some artists such as William Butterfield, the great architect of 19th-century churches, have deliberately avoided any mere prettiness. (And Butterfield, for one, was unquestionably successful in his effort.) The great danger in seeking beauty in music is that it becomes an effort to create only an effect. Some romantic composers of the last century fell into this trap; this may account for the fact that their works have been so popular in the choir repertory of many

---

[1]Copyright 1960, Christian Century Foundation. Reprinted by permission from the March 23, 1960 issue of *The Christian Century*, pp. 355-56.

churches. But much of this type of music is no longer considered to be of the highest type.

The relationship of beauty and common worship is highly ambiguous. The Bible does not praise beauty as an abstraction, and the often quoted text "O worship the Lord in the beauty of holiness" could be translated more accurately as "Worship the Lord in holy array" (or "in festal garments"). Beauty is certainly not the end of Christian worship, yet it tends to become such for many people. In *The Organization Man* William H. Whyte, Jr., points out that in one new community people listed music as one of the five most important factors in their choice of a church. The very attractiveness of good music makes it a dangerous accompaniment of common worship.

Perhaps more unfortunate is the relationship which choral music bears to congregational participation in worship. It has become apparent in almost every field of life that the specialist can do a better job than the amateur. Church music is no exception, and today we are witnessing a pattern previously acted out in the late Middle Ages—the development of professionalism in worship. Clearly a choir can sing much better than an untrained congregation, and there is a temptation to let the trained musicians carry a large portion of the service. Professionalism is a trend which affects all realms of church life, but nowhere is it so pernicious as in worship. Many churches have sprinkled their services with choral responses and choral amens, believing they have become more "liturgical" thereby. The result has been to make the services more complicated and perhaps more beautiful. But this is quite different from making them more liturgical, if the word be interpreted in its original sense as referring to the work of the people. Professionalized worship is actually less liturgical than nonprofessionalized because it reduces the congregation to a passive auditory role.

There is no reason, of course, why the choir cannot be used to encourage congregational singing of hymns and perhaps responses too. Some notable experiments have been tried in which trained choir members were scattered throughout the congregation with the intention of encouraging singing on the part of all worshipers. As usually constituted, however, choirs tend to play a substitutional role in worship. In their original role as the resident body of a cathedral or a monastic or collegiate church, choirs represented real congregational worship, since the singers included the entire worshiping community. Today the choir consists of only a portion of the worshipers, but it frequently monopolizes the congregation's role in worship.

A more serious charge against the presence of the choir in common worship is that listening to music may detract from the corporate quality of such worship. The essence of common worship is that all participate in it as one mind as well as one body. This means that common worship is, as its name indicates, worship in which the attention of all the people is centered upon the same concept made articulate or dramatized. In short, it is highly objective. Usually the congregation participates directly through hymn singing, reciting the creed, or hearing the word proclaimed. Meditation or contemplation, which are private and individual forms of worship, are not appropriate to common worship. The usual response to choral music, particularly anthems, is a subjective one, stimulating private worship rather than corporate worship. This response is particularly apt to occur when the words are difficult to understand (which is frequently the case), when they are in a foreign language, or when they are too trivial or doctrinally gauche to engage the common attention of the congregation. The sacred concert, which does not pretend to be the occasion of common worship, should be regarded as the proper occasion for choral music and private worship.

Finally, many Protestants seem quite unaware of the fact that austerity can be very compatible with common worship. Far from being opposed to Christian worship, austerity in music and the ornamentation of a church can help considerably in encouraging common worship instead of individual worship. It is most unfortunate that Protestants have so often confused the terms "liturgical" and "ornate." Some leaders of the contemporary liturgical movement have advocated a move towards an austerity based on theological principles. One leading Roman Catholic scholar has suggested removing from the church where mass is said many images, altars, stations and other such embellishments which stimulate private devotions.

Actually we have only to look at our own Protestant tradition to realize that there are good reasons for condemning the injudicious use of art forms. The Puritans took art so seriously that they realized it must be used carefully. When they rejected it in their worship (and they frequently retained it in their homes), they did so for theological reasons. There is, of course, a difference between austerity and barrenness; music should be used wheneer it will encourage common worship, particularly through the singing of hymns. But choral music, or any other kind, should be subject to a careful theological scrutiny. When a choir does not foster corporate worship, or when it actually impedes it, the choir is expendable. Even excellent music should be rejected if it detracts from the worship of the church. After all, a large portion of Protestantism worshiped for more than three centuries without choirs.

Howard D. McKinney

(1890-   )

As composer, author, and editor, Howard McKinney has experienced great changes in musical styles and attitudes within this century. The editorials he has written for the *Fischer Edition News*, an advertising pamphlet widely distributed to church musicians, have several times reflected his concern for the quality and future of religious music. In the present instance he compares musical change and the relaxation of liturgical practice, political unrest and cultural ferment. Among the several "little magazines" that are sent out regularly by publishing houses, principally to advertise the wares of each firm, the one edited by Dr. McKinney has shown the most consistently thoughtful analysis of the musical scene.

Winds of Change[1]

Most organists and choirmasters are so completely absorbed in their own tasks, so desperately concerned with their attempts to solve the problems that come up day by day, so busy with the planning necessary to carry on their weekly services — not to speak of the big seasonal ones at Christmas and Easter — that they have little time or inclination to sit down and reflect a bit on the problems of the world around them, a world torn with strife, clouded with doubt and beset with continuous argument. And this in spite of the fact that their whole future will depend upon the way these problems are tackled and the manner in which they may be solved.

It has now become perfectly evident that the nineteen-sixty decade marks a period of violent change in all fields of world activity — political, social, religious, and artistic. Western man finds himself in the midst of the debris of the old house he has been building for himself during the past five centuries, without

[1]Source, *Fischer Edition News*, Vol. XLV, No. 1 (September-October, 1967), pp. 1-6. Printed by permission of J. Fischer & Bro.

having a new one ready to move into. The political world is in the process of recovering from the disastrous effects of two world struggles within a period of twenty-five years, of breaking up old political alignments and forming new ones, and of trying to evaluate the relative merits of such opposing political concepts as capitalism and communism. The social world is attempting to prove the practical worth of democracy through measures aimed at rectifying injustices that have long been apparent in various sections of the world's societies, and providing some kind of more reasonable equilibrium between the rich and poor. In the religious world even such an historically conservative organization as the Roman Catholic Church has found it necessary to undergo profound changes in order to meet the demands of the present day, changes which no one could have contemplated only a few years ago. And the arts are now in the process of rejecting the concept of a culture based on the idea that reality consists of that which can be sensed, without finding what can be substituted in its place. They are in the midst of a transitional period that marks the end of one great creative epoch and the beginning of an era of uncertain, unknown experimentation, a transition that may well take at least a century.

In the swirling chaos which has resulted from these conflicts of ideas and these opposing social and political forces, it is natural that there be a sharp line of demarcation distinguishing the past from the future, the conservative from the radical, what may appear to be old-fashioned and dull, because based on the experience and traditions of the past, from the youthful experimentation and radical action suited to the necessities of today and the hopes for tomorrow. The church musician working in his own isolated situation, within the cloistered shelter of the choirloft, is apt to think that these distinctions are not present in his world and that the problems they invoke could not possibly affect his future. He could not be more mistaken! As a matter of fact, busy as he must be in two spheres of modern creative activity, he will become more and more involved in this growing conflict of ideas and it becomes obvious that his whole future, as well as that of the entire world of church music, will depend upon the way this conflict is resolved.

If we reduce this problem to its simplest and most immediate application, the question of the kind of church music that should be used in a service of worship, its answer depends, or should depend, upon what we mean by "worship," and what we consider the role of music to be in such services. And this, in turn, will depend upon the answer given to the one great fundamental theological question of the present: how do we speak, or think, or act about God — we who live in a technological society that is growing by leaps and bounds, and in the midst of scientific achievements undreamt of only a few years ago. It is this question of articulating religious faith in a life that must be lived in a scientific world, of making it clear and distinct and precise just what is meant by the concept of God, that provokes the questions that are now being raised by Protestants, Catholics, and Jews alike. And it is interesting to observe that in all these denominations the conservatives have tended to answer these questions by loudly re-affirming traditional beliefs, while the liberals demand "cultural analyses, social action and new institutional forms."

These disturbing questions were first clearly and forcefully defined some twenty years ago by the German Lutheran theologian, Dietrich Bonhoeffer, who posed them in a Nazi prison while awaiting death because of his implication in the attempted murder of Hitler. Because of the astounding growth of human and scientific knowledge, he said, the world no longer needs the hypothesis of God to explain its phenomena or justify its actions. Face to face with death, he realized that the world's beliefs have been reduced to only a very few ultimate questions such as the meaning of death or the presence of guilt. What are you going to say, he asked his professorial brethren, when these, too, become explainable without the hypothesis of God?

Ever since Bonhoeffer's death, theologians in all the Christian countries have been occupied with trying to answer his question. Prominent thinkers such as Tillich and Niebuhr have turned their attention to man's personal relationship to God in the life of the twentieth century. Such radical groups as the "death of God" theologians and the recent manifestations of "Pike's pique" are merely present-day examples of these attempts to rework Christian precepts and beliefs in the light of twentieth-century knowledge. In a very thoughtful book on this whole question of the future of belief, Dr. Leslie Dewart, a lay Roman Catholic theologian, offers an outline of the forms he thinks this problem of interpreting God in terms of present-day experience may follow. In the past, he says, the idea of a Christian God who not only spoke to man, but was also "made flesh" and took part in human history, and who, because of this omnipotence was considered a supreme being, was effectively communicated through the Greek concept of *logos* — the Word. Now, however, these concepts of God seem no longer tenable, and scientific and existential modes of communication have replaced the Greek one. Dr. Dewart argues that even though religious experience may prove to us that God does exist, we can no longer experience him as *being*, but rather as a presence that is a part of the history which man himself is shaping. So in the future he thinks it quite possible that Christian theology will not conceive of God as a person, or, indeed, a Trinity of persons, but rather as a presence. Concepts of omnipotence and eternity will give way to others such as historical possibility, freedom, or equality; "worship will become not the bended knee, but the rendering of ourselves to the presence of God." And it is likely, Dewart believes, that in the future some adequate substitute will have to be found for the traditional word *God*.

Even this truncated and hasty statement of the backgrounds of modern theological thinking, however, should show the church musician what his own problems are now and will be in the future. While he may not be entirely clear in his own mind as to the role that his music should play in the worship of the church he serves, he is even more uncertain as to the type of music he may be expected to provide in the services of the future. What will be the demands of his minister and congregation in the years to come? Will they be necessarily conservative or radical in their nature? Will those concerned with the musical program think of liturgical music and language as means to carry the "weight of glory which man should feel in the worship of God," means that necessarily are different from those used in every-day life and so suited to help man to a vision of God? If so, it will obviously be his duty to carry into his joy such enthusiasm for the best in liturgical music and language that will enable him to develop the means for producing this type of music. And so the organist and choirmaster will necessarily depend upon the great heritage of the past as well as the resources of the present for the kind of music that is supremely good and worthy of this purpose.

On the other hand, if the minister and congregation should be inclined to agree with the conclusions of the U.S. Bishop's Commission of Liturgical Procedure that, since different groupings of those assembled for worship respond to different styles of musical expression, the needs of those members of the faithful who do not possess cultural backgrounds or experience can best be met by a congenial musical experience that is somewhat liturgically slanted. For them, contemporary folk types of music or contemporary jazz procedures are perfectly legitimate means for expressing "joy before the Lord." And the church musician who serves this type of social action will be expected to furnish new institutional forms of music and liturgy, even though in so doing he may arouse the contempt of the conservatives. For, as one of these exponents of American mass programs has put it, "every time some David presumes to dance before the Lord, some cultural snob, like David's wife, will arise to call it undignified."

Some of the clergymen who think along these lines have been particularly emphatic in expressing themselves on the type of music which should be used during the Christmas season; and their utterances on this subject may be taken as characteristic of the whole so-called "radical school." The great tides of commercialism, anti-traditionalism and anti-humanism that have been sweeping the world today seem to be especially menacing during the season which celebrates this greatest of all Christian festivals, the period which in the past provided inspiration for some of our greatest religious music. Not only is the use of classic compositions of composers from Des Pres to Bach and Handel criticized by the radicals, but also, and especially, the traditional carols that have sprung up more or less spontaneously through the centuries and which suggest in their naive texts and sweet melodies the simple beauties of the Christmas story.

In the view of Rev. Malcolm Boyd, one of the most voluble representatives of these mods, as they like to call themselves, traditional carols are simply manifestations of the Wizard of Oz atmosphere that he feels stifles the churches at Christmas time and which blocks out the problems of the real world that Jesus came to serve in a setting of poinsettias, trees, and rows of candles. "Get them out! Forget the old meaningless carols. Write new contemporary ones and have the youngsters accompany them on a guitar or bass. Have the pastor preach the Christmas sermon wearing a sports shirt or maybe a sweat shirt. Have the choir wear everyday clothes, not red and black robes. Get rid of everything that separates the house of worship from the world where Christ was born."

The puzzled choirmaster and church musician does not have to agree with the extreme radicalism of such statements if he admits that they contain certain elements of just criticism. Any more than he has to accept the tenets of the traditionalists who pattern their liturgical procedures and their ideas of worship on the relatively static and archaic ideas of the past. Nor does he have to limit himself to the presentation of what, for want of a better term, might be called pop-folk music in order to feel himself to be representative of his time. What about the use of such strictly twentieth-century techniques as tone-rows and electronically generated sounds? Here, as well as in all similar problems of the future, he must face up to realities, decide upon what he really believes, and use every possible means to make his music a vital part of the worship of the church he serves.

Frank Cunkle

Criticism and evaluation of the arts often find themselves under various kinds of pressures, actual, implied, or imaginary. Will the music publisher withdraw his advertisement from the offending journal? Will the composer ask his friends to cancel their subscriptions? Will time prove the reviewer to be out of step with his age? Editors probably can multiply these questions into a sizeable list. It is refreshing, then, to find an editor who takes a firm stand in answering one of the burning questions about church music: who is to blame for its continuing low quality level? The intent of his answer is more significant than its content, for when the editorial in *The Diapason* approaches the question head-on, it is clear that he is willing to stand behind his convictions.

Invitation to Arson[1]

With all the sensational ferment, some moving, some silly, that is going on in our churches and in their music, many have expressed sincere questions as to whether the profession of church music or even the church itself has any future relevance. We have stated our belief in the potential of both the church and its music to achieve a meaningful tomorrow and we feel this fervently. But if we had nothing better or even other on which to base our hopes than the average run of choral and organ music from our publishers, we would sink into a deep despair indeed.

Music publishers, as we have pointed out again and again, select for publication what their experience convinces them has the best chance to sell. They have payrolls and printer's bills and rent and paper costs to meet. Only a few subsidized series for commercial publishers and a few university presses are prepared to issue music strictly on its merits, regardless of its chances to sell even a first printing.

The norm of contemporary church and organ music must be a

[1]Reprinted by permission from *The Diapason*, June, 1968.

fairly accurate yardstick for measuring the overall quality of American church music. If this is the music published, it follows that it must be the music bought and eventually the music played and sung. Old choir libraries cannot account for more than a small percentage. By this measurement one can seriously question the professional equipment, the motivation and, worst of all, the taste of a vast section of American church musicians.

There have been few months in the last 12 years when this writer has not gone carefully through a generous stack of new church music. The question immediately suggests itself: has there been an improvement? Among the more scholarly works from the past, editions have improved greatly. But in the general run of the *just written*, there has been, frankly, not only no improvement but in fact no change whatever.

Who is at fault for American church music publication missing its opportunity and often even failing to do its simple job? The publishers? We have already given that a clear NO. The schools? The buyers and users of the music we deplore must surely number many graduates of every major school of music. The congregations? Don't you believe it! They don't even notice; if they did, there might be many church musicians suddenly pursuing new careers. The composers? Church musicians in the very highest echelons are writing this stuff, lending their names and their reputations to material ground out by the yard and on a level which should make all of us blush.

Brahms was said to have destroyed much of his output as unworthy of the Brahms name. MacDowell may even have discarded To A Wild Rose as trivial and irrelevant. There is a story about Dukas committing all his unpublished manuscripts to a bonfire a few weeks before his death.

Perhaps the greatest stimulus to the march of American church music would be a few good bonfires in you know whose incinerators.

Dave Brubeck

(1920-   )

Widely known in connection with jazz, Dave Brubeck has achieved international acclaim both as composer and performer. When, in 1967, he disbanded the famous Dave Brubeck Quartet (organized in 1951) in order to devote more time to composition, there was a considerable stir in the ranks of musicians and listeners alike. When his oratorio, *The Light in the Wilderness,* was announced, a degree of skepticism was apparent, especially among those who were unaware of Brubeck's training in composition, briefly with Schoenberg and for a longer period with Milhaud. Since its initial performance in the early part of 1968, the work has had repeated exposure, has been published and recorded, and various opinions have been heard. Brubeck's program notes, written for the first performance, are at the same time a composer's estimate of his work and a statement of his religious convictions. Brubeck is speaking for his age and for himself in the text that is printed here; he attempts the same in his music. The degree of his success must be judged by the reader and the listener.

The Light in the Wilderness[1]

When people ask why a jazz musician should attempt to write an oratorio, they invariably want to know what "the persuasion" of my religious convictions is. To dispense with the last question first, although reared as a Presbyterian by a Christian Scientist mother who attended a Methodist church, and although this piece was written with the theological counsel of a Vedanta leader, a Unitarian minister, an Episcopalian bishop and several Jesuit priests, I am not affiliated with any church. Three Jewish teachers have been a great influence in my life—Irving Goleman, Darius Milhaud, and Jesus. I am a product of Judaic-Christian thinking. Without the complications of theological doctrine I wanted to understand what I had inherited in this world—both problems and answers—from that cultural heritage. This composition is, I suppose, simply one man's attempt to distill in his own thought and to express in his own way the essence of Jesus' teaching. In fact, at one point I considered titling this work "The Temptations and Teachings of Christ."

THE LIGHT IN THE WILDERNESS, Part I, takes as its text the temptations of Jesus, his message of hope to a suffering world, and the summation of his teaching in the commandment to love one another. The baptism of Jesus was the dramatic sign for his mission to begin—and it was Jesus the Teacher I wanted to understand—thus, the oratorio opens with this symbolic picture of man's spiritual rebirth.

If one wants to revolutionize the thinking of the world without destroying it, how does one begin? The temptation to rationalize one's compromising as a *means* to gain idealistic *ends* is the theme of the wilderness dialogue between Jesus and the devil. In the choral narrative I have given almost equal power to the scheming Tempter and the opening Voice from Heaven, both of which are written in 5/4 meter, to emphasize that in each of us (even Jesus) the tug of war between good and evil is never ending.

The symbolic significance of each temptation has been the source of much speculation. Everyone seems to understand *bread* (it's the jazz world's term for money). It's the most commonly used tool of power among men and nations. We should earnestly ponder the reasons why a starving Jesus rejected as unworthy the promise of fulfilled appetites. Later in his ministry, Jesus, out of compassion, did feed the hungry. The ethical questions raised by the first temptations are extremely relevant. Does one use man's insatiable appetite to gain power? Are we generous only when the granary is full? Does one give only when the recipient can repay, or when he can be useful to our purpose? In his later teaching Jesus answered these questions for us.

The second temptation is a test of faith, a sly challenge to the ego. I think Jesus refused the power of the *miracle* and the spectacular leap from the "pinnacle of the Temple" so that he could demonstrate in his humanity the greater power of love and compassion. Just as one should not use the physical appetites of man for gain, neither should one prey upon his fear of the supernatural.

Finally, the devil flashed before the eyes of Jesus the most tempting prize of all—*absolute power* to rule all nations and all peoples. Could such a prize enable Jesus to fulfill his selfless dream of perfection? Our world's history has been a continual demonstration of the corruption that accompanies power. Although Jesus was prepared ultimately to sacrifice his life, the devil's price for the earthly kingdom was far too dear. "For what does it profit a man to gain the whole world and lose his own soul?"

Jesus' rejection of all known approaches to power leaves for our consideration the one way the world has not fully tried. It was the one way Jesus chose 2000 years ago.

Jesus in the wilderness is only touched upon by the Synoptic gospels. Whatever went on in his mind during his solitary fast, it must have been a soul-searching beyond our imagination; and yet he must have asked basically the same question we all ask — *Who am I?* This lonely search is what I tried to express in FORTY DAYS, sung first as a quiet hymn, followed by an introspective instrumental passage, much in the style of a Bach chorale, in 5/4 meter.

When it was clear to Jesus who he was and what he must do, he emerged from the desert wilderness with the passionate cry to RETHINK! (for that is what "repent" means), to look at traditional teaching with new eyes, to hear God's word with new ears, to feel the wonder of life with the open senses of a child.

The revolutionary concept that the last shall be made first was his first major sermon. The chorus, acting sometimes as narrator and sometimes in the timeless role of the multitude, repeats the joyful promise of the Beatitudes, but in their expectant hope do not need Jesus' exhortation to RETHINK as the necessary prelude. Throughout the Beatitudes there is struggle between the solo voice of Jesus and the voice of the multitude. The chorus shouts of heavenly reward; Jesus counsels THINK! NOW! "The kingdom of God is within you." After the tumult the disciples are solemnly chosen. As each name is called (12 different notes for the 12 disciples) timpani beats portray the measured tread of footsteps. These simple men who answered Jesus' call, "Follow me" were destined to walk the face of the known world and alter the course of history. "The meek shall inherit the earth."

Jesus came, he said, not to destroy the law, but to fulfill it. The chorus of the faithful in 5/4 ostinato ask "Teach us, Master. What must we do to gain eternal life?" Like classroom children, they repeat the basic and familiar tenet: "Thou shalt love the Lord thy God with thy whole soul, with thy whole mind, with thy whole strength; and thy neighbor as thyself." Jesus adds: "Love your enemies." According to some religious scholars this commandment is the one new moral concept Jesus brought to the traditional code of the Jews. Although we have been told the minds of the East and West shall never meet, it fascinates me that Buddha, over 500 years before Jesus, considered the identical concept the crowning jewel of enlightenment.

The idiocy of the entire Christian world bent on fratricide rather than on brotherhood leads me to believe that we have missed the whole point of Jesus' life. I puzzled as a young soldier twenty-five years ago (as I do now) at Christians who can still think in terms of "the enemy," forgetting that devout prayers are being offered to the One God from both sides of the battle. In God's eyes can there be an enemy?

A peaceful and merciful world seems to me as credible as Hitler's army of hate. We can surely enlighten and prepare for a cause more natural to man's spirit. Chaplains reported during World War II that almost every man in his solitude was a pacifist, and selfless sacrifices to save others were common. The dualism of man is apparent throughout history. Some of the bloodiest chapters have been written in the name of religion, and on the other hand, some of history's most enlightened regimes have been controlled by the military (Europe and Japan following World War II). General Omar Bradley said,

> We have grasped the mystery of the atom and rejected the Sermon on the Mount. The world has achieved brilliance without wisdom, power without conscience. Ours is a world of nuclear giants and ethical infants. We know more about war than we know about peace, more about killing than we know about living.

All men in their highest idealism recognize the nobility and love in a Christ, or a Buddha, or a Socrates. Aren't the questioning youth of today—these modern uncouth prophets crying in the wilderness—truly the sons and daughters of our own aspiration? Aren't they rudely reminding us of the torch of idealism we have allowed to dim?

Using a jagged twelve-note theme that stresses the difficulty of the commandments to love your enemies, Jesus explains what it means in terms of daily existence. He does not plead for love in harmonious, sentimental tones, but sings more of a battle cry for courage to face the war with self. This section is based on three twelve-note themes. The first is stated in the form of a command (in 3/4 time) with an antiphonal response from the chorus, followed by a method (in 4/4), a corollary in the Oriental manner of "rules of conduct," which helps one to obey the command. The same pattern is also used in the antiphonal response of the chorus.

Love your enemies. (3/4)	Do good to those who hate you. (4/4)
Bless those who curse you.	Pray for those who abuse you.
To him who strikes you on the cheek	Offer the other also.
From him who takes away your cloke	do not withhold your coat as well.

The second twelve-note theme is the Golden Rule: "And as you wish that men would do to you, do so to them."

The third theme, "If you love those that love you, what credit is that to you?" introduces rhythmic patterns of growing complexity.

"He sends his rain on the just and unjust; makes his sun rise on the evil. He makes his sun rise on the good. Do not judge and you shall not be judged. Do not condemn and you will not be condemned. Forgive and you will be forgiven. Give and it is given to you. Good measure, pressed down, shaken together, running over, will be put in your lap."

In the twelve extended cadential bars, which is the final statement of the main theme, "the measure that ye give will be the measure you get back" is musically demonstrated by adding one beat to each measure of the theme, "Love your enemies. Do good to those who hate you." Meanwhile, the chorus, also adding a beat to each measure, recapitulates the lessons Christ has just taught them. A variety of musical styles has been used freely throughout the piece (since Christian teaching is for all time), but it is even more evident in "Love Your Enemies" with its musical collage of quick jumps from modern to modal, Middle Eastern to country hoe-down, jazz, rock and roll to martial drums.

Part II deals primarily with questions of faith and man's place in the universe. A lesson from the temptations is formulated in the opening solo "What does it profit a man if he gain the whole world and lose his own soul?" This is followed by a simple setting of the 24th Psalm, picturing man serenely at peace with nature. As the Psalmist's text moves from peaceful oneness of creation to questions about our uniquely human condition, the writing becomes more complex. Using as a departure point the text "This is the generation of them that seek him," the choir becomes the voice of all lost and seeking generations in their confused and sometimes fruitless search for meaning.

Jesus blesses all those who seek with a promise of spiritual peace.

"Let not your heart be troubled, ye believe in God" was meant to be part of a service dedicated to the memory of my young nephew, Philip, whose sudden death in May, 1965, profoundly affected our family. From the initial piece, a testimony of faith, grew the idea of an oratorio to be dedicated to Philip and my own children's generation. Actually, the idea of writing such a piece has been growing in my mind for many years. As a child I did not question the literal meaning of the many mansions in my Father's house. I am not sure of the true meaning of this passage now (although I'm sure the many questions are as figurative as Buddha's many ladders to heaven), but the child's faith remains.

Jesus' final solo "Yet a little while is the light with you" is the plea of our Christian heritage to walk while we still have the light, lest the darkness come upon us.

If the first life on earth was a unicellular blob, its formation was no less of a miracle than Adam, and all of life is of common descent. In the totality of the universe our 20th century concepts are scarcely less primitive than the archaic text of Psalm 148, a magnificent hymn of all creation and the almighty Creator. PRAISE YE THE LORD! is an unquestioning affirmation of all life in all forms. I have chosen to close with this Psalm because like the ancient psalmist, my religious faith is rooted in awe at the infinitude of creation.

When I see signs of the times in the streets, hear the songs of social protest, read the poetry of youth, they seem to portend a new era, perhaps even a new age. The Christian world had its age of Faith in the dim past when Faith is all we had. The age of Hope was ushered in by the Enlightenment and the optimistic expansion of Western (hence, Christian) civilization. In the accelerated pace of history, will the 21st century be known as the Age of Love?

This is the generation of them that seek him.

Ralph Thibodeau

It is fitting that one of the closing sections in this anthology deals with music of the Roman Catholic Church, for it was there that musical traditions were first established for Christianity, and it was there that repeated attempts were made to prevent the intrusion of secular elements, to preserve the dignity of worship in music. Ralph Thibodeau, an associate professor of music at Del Mar College, Corpus Christi, Texas, sees the collapse of the traditional bastions not in the use of vernacular texts — for which no music existed in usable form — as some had feared, but in a permissiveness fostered by authority that lacked musical knowledge or interest. To a great extent, the phenomenon parallels what was seen in the Church of England near the end of the eighteenth century, not in the musical result, but in the attitudes of the ruling clergy.

Threnody for Sacred Music, 1968
or,
The People of God Have Been Had[1]

The sign at the entrance to Dante's hell reads, *Lasciate ogni speranza voi ch'entrate:* all hope abandon, ye who enter here. For anyone even dispassionately interested in Catholic sacred music, this might seem an appropriate graffito to be scrawled on the church doors. Only perhaps the original Iconoclasts and the Cromwellians could match the present anti-artistic movement in the American Church.

Whatever impact the "death of God" may have had on Catholicism, it is apparent that it has been paralleled by the death of sacred music. May we who survive be forgiven if we make our threnody.

It is now five years since the promulgation of the conciliar

[1]Reprinted from *Commonweal,* LXXXIX/11 (December 13, 1968), 378-79 by permission of Commonweal Publishing Co., Inc.

196

Constitution on the Sacred Liturgy, long enough to see shattered the dreams of the liturgists for a noble singing Church. Sacred art music has become the victim of an unwritten Declaration of Irrelevance.

This may not seem unusual in a period of revolutionary turmoil, and at first glance the artistic problem becomes insignificant when held up to the general problems of birth control, poverty, racism and war. But to ignore the troubles of sacred art would be to beg the question. Only in the narrowest sense can we cite revolution as the cause of our neglect. There are no barricades before the church doors, and there is no persecution. We are still filling the churches for Sunday Mass. But what of our singing and our community?

In the name of the "People of God," the amorphous mass of Catholic humanity for whom, ostensibly, the liturgists commit their Puritanical depredations, we have now been reduced to a non-community of non-singers performing non-music. We have made two artistic compromises in our Church music: we have tried cheap vernacular settings of Mass-texts, and vernacular hymns; and we have tried, in the name of youth, rock and folk music. Both compromises have been found invalid, because both have failed as the vaunted panacea for our musical and liturgical woes. The main reason for the failure is obvious. The musicians who might have helped have not only been left out of the deliberations, they have actually been defenestrated, like so many Renaissance fall guys, their leadership repudiated by ill-advised pastors.

While Catholics have been eager to hear and speak the Good Word in their own language, they have by no means been eager to sing. And without leadership they will not sing. Without the strong choirs and professional organists and directors of the Protestant tradition, popular participation in singing, whatever its promised glories, is doomed to failure. It's as simple as that. If anyone has any doubts, he has only to go to Mass, and then attend a service in a normal Protestant church some Sunday morning. The contrast is enough to make men weep.

People, God's or otherwise, get sick of the same four hymns week after week, and of the insipid playing on instruments that pass for organs, and of poor, leaderless sheep floundering around in search or a tune.

As some day it may happen that a solution may be sought, I've got a little list of musical offenders, and they'd none of 'em be missed. There's the amusical commentator who fails to lead; the mountebank song leader who leads astray; and three varieties of organ operative: the lady pianist; the student prodigy (also a pianist); and the retired accordion player. All three of the latter have in common an uncommon penchant for pulling the vibrato stop, and their lack of even an elementary pedal technique suggests that they may have no feet. In some cases their mauling of the manuals suggests that they play in mittens.

As a result of the poor response of congregations to ill-conceived efforts at having them sing, there has been created in the Church a musical vacuum. Into it have rushed legions of litkooks, with priestlings in the van. With no knowledge of music, and, regrettably, no real culture of any sort, they have rushed in where angels fear to tread with their rock-and-roll and manufactured-for-profit "folk music." In both congregational hymn singing and "folk" Masses, the rationale of the incompetent authority has been to cater to the Lowest Common Denominator, to "give the people what they want." And just as in television a vast wasteland has been created by referring all decisions to pander[er]s to the L.C.D., so we need not be surprised that the process has created a second cultural wasteland in the churches. There is little artistic, or spiritual, difference between the Flying Nun and the "People's Mass."

Note this resume of a "Rite of Reconciliation" at the latest liturgical conference last summer (*Commonweal.* Sept. 20, 1968). "The rite, cast largely in the form of a light show complete with multiple screens, a psychedelic rock group known as 'The Mind Garage,' free peanuts and free-flowing wine, was a tour de force (marred only by a vulgar preacher) that excited many, bewildered others, and drove some screaming from the hall."

The "rite" was not a Mass, but the idea of a good folk Mass seems to be to celebrate the joyful news of Redemption with a carnival, with appropriate carnival music, banners, balls and balloons. We have seemed to abandon the Ordinary and the Proper of the Mass for the extraordinary and the improper, all in the name of a rather nebulous dogma that youth must be served, and all the rest of the good "People of God" who are young at heart. And now that rock-and-roll has pretty well had its day, the question inevitably arises, when this stuff goes out of style, where in the hell, literally, are we? With hillbilly coming on strong, how long will it be before we are regaled with *Lord, have mercy* to the tune of "Tears in my Ears," with souped-up fiddles swooping through graceless portamentos, while adenoidal voices make a travesty of the by-then ersatz texts of the *Missa Wilhelmi de Montibus?*

The inescapable fact is that the "People of God" have been had. Either they listen to the drivel that passes for congregational participation at the normal parish Mass, or they go with the kids to the Hootenanny Mass, to have their ears assaulted and their minds insulted.

Given the present state of the musical culture, it is amazing that there are any pockets of artistic music left. But there are some, and their rationale is the psychological truth that the perception of musical beauty can provide a legitimate emotional response to enhance the spiritual message of the Mass. The persons in position of authority who have brought sacred music to a 2000-year nadir have failed to grasp that truth. It is up to those who can see to lend their sight to the blind, to demand that they no longer lead the other blind into a vicious circle.

I think it is possible to agree with the premises contained here, and still appreciate all the efforts of all the liturgists and others to make the Church more relevant to man in our day. But in the specifically liturgical matters, in which they are granted expertise, they often seem not so much healers of souls as witch doctors, prescribing nostrums and incantations for the worship of the Lord. Perhaps in the present turmoil it is impossible to retain the old structures, literally or figuratively, of the Church. This will have to be seen. But if we be permitted yet to seek beauty in the architecture, art and music of the Church, if we may yet worship in the temple, then, in all good sense, let us kick out the witch doctors and call back the musicians. The honest alternative is a return to the silent church.

One need not be a complete Gaullist to advert, in the present connection, to the general's great *mot: réforme. oui. chienlit. non.*

Stephen Koch

By mid-twentieth-century church attendance had declined; traditional church practice, if not completely rejected by its former followers, had been subordinated. The number of young people flowing into the membership of the established church had been diminished; youth had been contaminated by its easy access to entertainment, largely through the convenience of television. Pastors, youth leaders, church musicians, turned toward the popular idioms in attempts tooo the youth back to the church. Pop-gospel music, folk-rock, and message musicals were among the experiments, and one of the directions these led in America was toward a staged musical show. It was inevitable that someone should find the key that put this idiom into show business, onto Broadway and into the transient but profitable area of arrangements for folk-rock youth groups, high-school choristers, and marching bands.

Whether the resulting shows are properly classified as religious seems beside the point. The popular taste embraced such productions, and the name of the Deity was raised in a fashion and in musical idioms that a few decades earlier would have seemed obscene. Appropriately, then, the final word on musical shows with religious stories, but without any evangelistic or worshipful function, comes from a theater critic rather than a church musician or theologian. Stephen Koch compared three highly successful works of the 1970s as theater pieces, and properly so, for they were written for the theater and it was there they found their public. Expensive, slick, and professional, they have not become the substitute for the church, but they have become, for the present, its principal surrogate.

God on Stage[1]

Religion has reached Broadway on some strange trajectories, but strangeness has not kept this particular descending dove from landing on the jackpot. A secular, liberal postwar generation raises its children in Stevensonian skepticism only to discover them seeking not ethical culture and the rectitude of tolerance but

[1]Reprinted from *WORLD Magazine.* 9/12/72, pp. 58, 60-61 by permission. Copyright ©1972 *World Magazine.*

high — in every sense — mysticism and an eventual return to Jesus. Or is that in fact what has happened? I suspect understanding the phenomenon requires some complex discussion of what nobody in America wants to discuss — to wit, its class system — and while awaiting the sociological returns, I leave to Billy Graham how "real" may be my contemporaries' return to the fold, pausing only to observe that in America neither ethical culture nor mysticism nor the Man of Sorrows himself ever really interferes with Show Biz. The wave began a mere two years ago when two obscure young Britons, Andrew Lloyd Webber and Tim Rice, composed their rock opera *Jesus Christ Superstar*, unexpectedly creating one of the most successful albums of our time. It is a tribute to their inspiration, albeit a tribute of a depressing kind, that *Superstar* has sailed with such speed directly to the grandest Broadway has to offer, that Jesus now finds himself in those hallowed regions where Ethel Merman once walked. Not to be outdone, Leonard Bernstein has in record time installed his trendy pick-up, *Mass*, in that same Metropolitan Opera which waited thirty years to stage Berg's *Lulu*. We have a new beatitude, tacked on right after "Blessed are ye. . . ."It is, "There's no business like show business."

. . . .

In the meantime, between *Superstar* and *Mass* emerged a much more modest production, *Godspell*, which was, however, not so modest as to fail quickly to achieve successes ordinarily undreamt of off-Broadway: much Johnny Carson coverage, a pretty successful album, a smash single ("Day by Day") and advance box-office sales which make the producers suspect they have nothing to do but count money until their Hero at last sees fit to come again. By general consent, including my own, *Godspell* is hands down the best theater the current wave has produced. Apparently Mr. Bernstein thought so too; at any rate, he promptly raided the production to hire Mr. Stephen Schwartz, its lyricist, to write for him *Mass*, forgetting that Mr. Schwartz has cribbed most of *Godspell* from a talent unavailable even to Mr. Bernstein, namely Saint Matthew. Mr. Schwartz had thus become the only lyricist in memory, indeed the only writer of any kind since Harriet Beecher Stowe, with some claim to doing his work with assistance from God. Unfortunately, circumstances forced him to do *Mass* entirely on his own. The results make clear that God's help is something Mr. Schwartz very much needs.

The word, I think, is by now out about *Mass:* Mr. Bernstein had
found the latest and decided to elevate it to higher levels. Well, if
this absolutely synthetic (in the worst sense) long-awaited
masterpiece, composed of equally lavish parts of p.r., high *culturati*
cash, that old Kennedy Glow, bad music and sententious
cast-of-thousands staging which would have embarrassed de Mille
and seemed muddy and overblown at Radio City Music Hall — if
this, as I was saying, is elevation, we would do well to keep our
feet on the ground, preferably by walking briskly away. Robert
Craft has already written his musical opinion elsewhere; I defer to
it entirely. For my part, *Mass* held me rapt with grim fascination
at the spectacle of Mr. Bernstein's two halves fighting it out: the
amazingly gifted musician vying in schizzy desperation with the
greatest cultural careerist of the century. Guess who handily won
the fight.

I recommend *Jesus Christ Superstar* with a kind of reluctance,
though by the time Tom O'Horgan, who staged what is basically
all staging, consolidates his career as Absolute Lord of Broadway
(maybe next season, if it hasn't already occurred), I may curse my
words. For I'm not sure I altogether welcome O'Horgan's smoothly
spectacular showmanship, though smoothly spectacular it assuredly
is. Mr. O'Horgan is blessed with the interesting combination of a
thoroughly chic and thoroughly vulgar mind, exactly the kind of
mind on which Broadway has always lavished the cornucopia of its
most intoxicating favors; and *Jesus Christ Superstar* is therefore
recommended as *the* example of what American show biz is
currently all about. At first blush — the only blush most showmen
care about — the chic casts a fig leaf over the vulgarity and the
show sails on.

. . . .

Both *Mass* and *Superstar* have everything on their side, sustained
by talent, influence, publicity, chic, fame, endless technical
resources, endless money, and budgets that stop at nothing. They
have absolutely everything except a genuine artistic idea. And at
the risk of pomposity, one clears one's throat to remark that that
last little item is a *sine qua non* without which anything on a stage
is finally as resounding brass.

. . . .

BIBLIOGRAPHY

Alcock, John. *A Morning and Evening Service*. . . . London: Printed for the Author and Jno. Johnson, 1752.

Anderson, Emily, ed. *The Letters of Mozart & His Family*. 3 vols. London: Macmillan and Co., 1938.

Arnold, Samuel, ed. *Cathedral Music*. 4 vols. London: For the Editor, 1790.

Beethoven, Ludwig van. *Beethoven's Letters (1790-1826)*. Trans. by Lady Wallace. 2 vols. London: Longmans, Green, and Co., 1866.

Billings, William. *The Continental Harmony, containing, A Number of Anthems, Fuges, and Chorusses, in several Parts*. Boston: Isaiah Thomas and Ebenezer T. Andrews, 1794. Reprint ed. by Hans Nathan. Cambridge: The Belknap Press of Harvard University Press, 1961.

Brownson, Oliver. *Select Harmony*. New Haven: Thomas and Samuel Green, 1783.

Brubeck, Dave. Program notes to *The Light in the Wilderness*. Delaware Water Gap, Pa.: Shawnee Press, 1968.

Burney, Charles. The Present State of Music in Germany, the Netherlands, and United Provinces . . . 2 vols.; 2nd ed., corrected; London: T. Becket and Co., 1775.

Buszin, Walter. "Luther on Music." *The Musical Quarterly* 32/1 (January, 1946): 81-82.

Chase, Gilbert. *America's Music: From the Pilgrims to the Present*. 2d ed. rev. New York: McGraw-Hill Book Company, 1966.

Colles, H. C. *Essays and Lectures*. London: Humphrey Milford; Oxford University Press, 1945.

Cox, John Edmund, ed. *Miscellaneous Writings and Letters of Thomas Cranmer*. 2 vols. Cambridge: The University Press, 1846.

Cunkle, Frank. "Invitation to Arson." *The Diapason* (June, 1968): 16.

Daniel, R. B. *Chapters on Church Music*. London: Elliott Stock, 1894.

David, Hans T., and Mendel, Arthur, eds. *The Bach Reader*. New York: W. W. Norton & Company, 1966.

Davison, Archibald T. *Protestant Church Music in America*. Boston: E. C. Schirmer Music Co., 1933.

Eastcott, Richard. *Sketches of the Origin, Progress and Effects of Music, with an Account of the Ancient Bards and Minstrels*. Bath: S. Hazard, 1793.

Evelyn, John. *The Diary of John Evelyn*. Edited by E. S. de Beer. 6 vols. Oxford: Clarendon Press, 1955.

Ferretti, Rt. Rev. Abbot Paul M., comp. *Papal Documents on Sacred Music*. New York: Society of St. Gregory of America, 1939.

Froude, J. A. *Life and Letters of Erasmus*. New York: Charles Scribner's Sons, 1895.

Grove's Dictionary of Music and Musicians. 5th ed. Edited by Eric Blom. 10 vols. New York: St. Martin's Press, 1954-61.

Hackett, Maria. *A brief account of cathedral and collegiate schools* . . . . London: J. Nichols and son, 1827.

Hastings, Thomas. ["An Address"]. In *Proceedings of the American Musical Association . . ..* New York: Saxton & Miles, 1845.

Hawkins, Sir John. *A General History of the Science and Practice of Music.* London: Novello, 1853.

Hayes, William. "Rules necessary to be observed by all Cathedral-Singers in this Kingdom." *The Gentleman's Magazine, and Historical Chronicle* 35 (May, 1765): 213-14.

Jocelin, Simeon. *The Chorister's Companion.* New Haven: Jocelin and Doolittle, [1782].

Koch, Stephen. "God on Stage." *WORLD Magazine* 9/12/72: 58-61.

Lowe, Edward. *A Short Direction for the Performance of Cathedrall Service.* Oxford: William Hall, 1661.

Luther, Martin. *Liturgy and Hymns.* Vol. 53 of *Luther's Works.* Edited by Ulrich S. Leupold. Philadelphia: Fortress Press, 1965.

Lyon, James. *Urania or a choice Collection of Psalm-Tunes, Anthems and Hymns From the most approv'd Authors, with some Entirely New . . ..* [Philadelphia: 1761].

Mace, Thomas. *Musick's Monument . . ..* 1676. Reprint. Paris: Éditions du centre national de la recherche scientifique, 1958.

Mason, Lowell. *Musical Letters from Abroad.* New York: Mason Brothers, 1854. Reprint. New York: Da Capo Press, 1967.

McKinney, Howard D. "Winds of Change." *Fischer Edition News* 44/1 (September-October, 1967): 1-6.

Mellen, John. *Religion Productive of Music.* Boston: Isaiah Thomas, 1773.

Mendelssohn, Felix. *Letters of Felix Mendelssohn Bartholdy from 1883 to 1847.* Translated by Lady Wallace. London: Longmans, Green, and Co., 1885.

Morley, Thomas. *A Plaine and Easie Introduction to Practicall Musicke.* 1597. Reprint edited by R. Alec Harman. New York: W. W. Norton and Co., [1953?].

Mozart Pilgrimage, A.: Being the Travel Diaries of Vincent & Mary Novello in the year 1829. Transcribed and compiled by Nerina Medici di Marignano. Edited by Rosemary Hughes. London: Novello & Co., 1955.

Naumann, Emil. *The History of Music.* Translated by F. Praeger. Edited by Rev. Sir F. A. Gore Ouseley. 2 vols. London: Cassel & Company, [1886].

Page, John. *Harmonia Sacra.* 3 vols. London: For the Editor, 1800.

Pepys, Samuel. *The Diary of Samuel Pepys.* Edited by Henry B. Wheatley. 1893. Reprint (2 vols.). New York: Random House, n.d.

Ravenscroft, Thomas. *The Whole Booke of Psalmes.* 2d ed. London; Thomas Harper, 1633.

Reese, Gustave. *Music in the Renaissance.* New York: W. W. Norton and Co., 1954; rev. ed., 1959.

Rimbault, Edward F., ed. *The Old Cheque-Book or Book of Remembrance of the Chapel Royal from 1561 to 1744.* 1872. Reprint. New York: Da Capo Press, 1966.

*Roger North on Music: Being a Selection of his Essays written during the years,
c.1695-1728.* Transcribed from the Manuscripts and edited by John
Wilson. London: Novello and Co., 1959.

Scholes, Percy A., ed. *Dr. Burney's Musical Tours in Europe.* 2 vols.
London: Oxford University Press, 1959.

Seely, Raymond. ["An Address"]. In *Proceedings of the American
Musical Association . . ..*New York: Saxton & Miles, 1845.

Sonneck, O. G. "A Survey of Music in America." In *Suum Cuique:
Essays in Music.* New York: G. Schirmer, 1916.

Stanford, C. V. *Studies and Memories.* London: Archibald Constable and
Co., 1908.

Statutes of Lincoln Cathedral. Edited by Henry Bradshaw and Chr.
Wordsworth. Cambridge: University Press, 1897.

Strunk, Oliver. *Source Readings in Music History.* New York: W. W.
Norton and Co., 1950.

Thibodeau, Ralph. "Threnody for Sacred Music, 1968: or, The People of
God Have Been Had." *Commonweal* 89/11 (December 13,
1968): 378-79.

Tudway, Thomas. "A Collection of the Most Celebrated Services and
Anthems . . .." British Museum MSS Harley 7337-7342.

Walter, Thomas. *The Grounds and Rules of Musick Explained: Or an Introduction to the Art of Singing by Note. Fitted to the meanest Capacities.*
Boston: Printed by J. Franklin for S. Gerrish, 1721.

_____ *The Sweet Psalmodist of Israel: A Sermon Preach'd at the Lecture
held in Boston, by the Society for promoting Regular and Good Singing,
and for reforming the Depravations and Debasements our Psalmody labours
under, in Order to introduce the proper and true Old Way of Singing.*
Boston: Printed by J. Franklin for S. Gerrish, 1722.

Wesley, Samuel Sebastian. *A Few Words on Cathedral Music and the Musical
System of the Church, with a Plan of Reform.* London: J. & J. Rivington, *et al.,* 1849. Reprint. New York: Hinrichsen Edition,
1961.

White, James F. "Church Choir: Friend or Foe?" *The Christian Century*
(March 23, 1960): 355-56.

Whole Booke of Psalmes Faithfully Translated into English Metre, The.
1640. Reprint. Chicago: The University of Chicago Press, 1956.

Wienandt, Elwyn A., and Young, Robert H. *The Anthem in England and
America.* New York: The Free Press, 1970.

Index

Absence from choir, 39-40, 70-71
  penalties for, 39-40
A cappella performance, 113, 117, 166
  Berlin Dom-Chor, 138, 140
Addenbrooke, Rev. Dr., 69
Ainsworth Psalter, 33
Albert Hall, London, 151
Alcock, John (1715-1806), 69, 69n.
Aldrich, Henry (1647-1710), 102
Alexander the Great, 109
Allegri, Gregorio (1582-1652), 82, 85
American Musical Convention, 123, 125
Anderson, Emily, 78n., 79n.
Anthem, 121, 123, 171, 180
  American, 136
  arranged from opera 171
  coronation, 22, 23
  English, 39, 57, 75, 94, 95, 101,
    102, 146, 152, 155
  solo, 102
Anthem (=antiphon), 11, 14
Antiphon, 42, 143, 144, 165, 166
Arnold, Samuel (1740-1802), 94, 94n.,
  95
Attire, choral, 39
Attwood, Thomas (1765-1838), 130

Bach family, 154
Bach, Johann Sebastian (1685-1750), 61,
  116, 117, 122, 128, 133, 136,
  154, 155, 186
Bach Reader, The, David and Mendel, 61
Balls, music publisher, 139
Bands
  indoors, 167
  outdoors, 168
Barnard, John (fl. 1640), 94
Barrel-organ, 147
Basso continuo, 57
Bay Psalm Book, 28
Bauer, Pastor, 121
Bayer, Nikolaus, 80n.
Beard, Mr., 75n.
Beethoven, Ludwig van (1770-1827),
  112-14, 157
Bellini, Vincenzo (1801-1835), 143
Benedict XIV, Pope, 67
Benevoli, Orazio (1605-1672), 85
Bennett, William Sterndale (1816-
  1875), 154

Berg, Alban (1885-1935), 201
Berlin, 136
  Singakademie, 112, 113
Berlioz, Hector (1803-1869), 143, 174
Bernstein, Leonard (1918-   ), 201-02
Billings, William (1746-1800), 86
  107, 107n.
Black List, Society of St. Gregory, 160
Blom, Eric (1888-1959), 38n.
Bonhoeffer, Dietrich (1906-1945), 184
Boyce, William (1710-1779), 82, 94, 95,
  130
Boyd, Rev. Malcolm (1923-   ), 186
Bradley, General Omar, 193
Bradshaw, Henry (1831-1886), 11n.
Brady, Nicholas (1659-1726), 98n.
Brahms, Johannes (1833-1897), 177, 189
Brief account of cathedral and collegiate
    schools, A, Hackett, 69
Brown, Dr., 106n.
Brownson, Oliver, 86, 86n.
Brubeck, Dave (1920-   ), 190
Brunetti, Gaetano (ca. 1740-1808), 79,
  79n.
Buddha, 193
Burney, Charles (1726-1814), 81, 81n.,
  97, 106n., 148
Buszin, Walter (1899-1973), 5n.
Butterfield, William (1814-1900), 178
Byrd, William (1543-1623), 85, 154, 174

Caeremoniale Episcoporum, 166, 167
Caldara, Antonio (1670-1736), 85
Canonical Hours, 42, 67
Cantata, 123, 166
Cardinal Patri, 143
Carrissini, probably Carissimi, Giacomo
    (1605-1674), 102
Carson, Johnny, 201
Castrati, 60, 79, 80
Cathedrals, 130-35, 164
Cathedral Music
  Arnold, 94
  Boyce, 130
Cathedral music and practice, 36-37, 48,
    70-71, 75, 94, 101, 128, 146,
    154, 178
Ceccarelli, Francesco, 79n.
Cecilian Movement, 143
Chantor; see Choirmaster

207

Never before in history have changes occurred as rapidly as in the past decade. Music for the church, in common with nearly every other aspect of our culture, has undergone significant but often disturbing change . . . in its styles, in its functions, in the attitudes of the people who perform it and listen to it. Understanding these changes is easier if we know the viewpoints of the past.

Opinions on Church Music will help the reader do just that. In a representative selection of letters, essays, sermons, memoirs, dedications, prefaces, and other documents taken from the writings of musicians, critics, historians, clergymen, and the lay public, this anthology reflects a wide range of reactions to the musical scene as it touches upon the church.

From Erasmus's criticism of choirboys to Stephen Koch's evaluation of *Jesus Christ Superstar* and *Godspell*, Dr. Wienandt has brought into focus a picture of the changing course of music with a religious message.